STUDIES IN ECONOMICS AND
POLITICAL SCIENCE

I0127684

Volume 11

THE LEGISLATIVE PROCESS
IN GREAT BRITAIN

THE LEGISLATIVE PROCESS
IN GREAT BRITAIN

S. A. WALKLAND

Routledge
Taylor & Francis Group

LONDON AND NEW YORK

First published in 1968 by George Allen & Unwin Ltd

This edition first published in 2022
by Routledge
4 Park Square, Milton Park, Abingdon, Oxon OX14 4RN

and by Routledge
605 Third Avenue, New York, NY 10017

Routledge is an imprint of the Taylor & Francis Group, an informa business

British Library Cataloguing in Publication Data
A catalogue record for this book is available from the British Library

ISBN: 978-1-03-212459-9 (Set)
ISBN: 978-1-00-322951-3 (Set) (ebk)
ISBN: 978-1-03-213011-8 (Volume 11) (hbk)
ISBN: 978-1-03-213019-4 (Volume 11) (pbk)
ISBN: 978-1-00-322727-4 (Volume 11) (ebk)

DOI: 10.4324/9781003227274

Publisher's Note
The publisher has gone to great lengths to ensure the quality of this reprint but points out that some imperfections in the original copies may be apparent.

Disclaimer
The publisher has made every effort to trace copyright holders and would welcome correspondence from those they have been unable to trace.

THE LEGISLATIVE PROCESS IN GREAT BRITAIN

S. A. Walkland

*Department of Political Theory
and Institutions*
University of Sheffield

London
GEORGE ALLEN AND UNWIN LTD
RUSKIN HOUSE MUSEUM STREET

FIRST PUBLISHED IN 1968

SECOND IMPRESSION 1969

© *George Allen and Unwin Ltd., 1968*

SBN 04 320060 5 paperbound edition
SBN 04 320048 6 clothbound edition

PRINTED IN GREAT BRITAIN
in 10 point Plantin type
BY WILLMER BROTHERS LIMITED
BIRKENHEAD

CONTENTS

ACKNOWLEDGEMENTS

The author is grateful to Dr Malcolm Anderson, of the University of Warwick, and to Professor Bernard Crick, of the University of Sheffield, for reading the manuscript and making many constructive suggestions. They have, of course, no responsibility for any errors or omissions which are still obvious.

INTRODUCTION

Studies of British government are peculiarly prone to be written in terms of formal constitutional notions associated with eighteenth- and nineteenth-century political developments. Concepts such as the legislative supremacy of Parliament, and the 'rule of law', useful in limited ways, still confuse students attempting to gain a balanced perspective of the workings of the modern British governmental system. In this short book the author has tried to look at one important process unhampered by received notions about British Parliamentary government, and to set out the major determinants of policy-making by legislative means. Much of the background for this study has been derived from the general analyses of British government and politics which have been made by such writers as Samuel Beer, Richard Rose and Harry Eckstein. The author owes a large debt to these authorities, and to a number of other scholars who have worked in this field. Wherever possible, full attribution has been made.

The book begins with an analysis of governmental activities in terms of the main procedures that are available in the governmental system for decision-making. In the author's view this is a much more revealing categorization than attempts to differentiate governmental activities by reference to the kinds of decision which result from them. When applied to the history of the legislative process, it reveals the different legislative procedures which at times have been dominant in Britain, and their relationship to particular stages in the political and administrative development of the country. Chapter I shows, briefly, how in the nineteenth century the procedures of Private Bill legislation gave way, because of changed administrative and political circumstances, to legislation by Public General Act, and how in this century subordinate legislation made by Government Departments has become the characteristic regulatory instrument of a society which has developed politically to the stage where it needs comparatively few major adjustments to its organization, but much in the way of minute and technical oversight of its activities.

Chapter II sets out broadly the sources of legislative policy in Britain. A developed society is characterized by a marked diffusion of the sources of political power. At the same time the British political executive is strong enough to be able to assert its own priorities, and legislative policy-making is explained in terms of the relationships which have emerged between pressure groups representing special interests, Government Departments and the Cabinet.

Chapters III and IV deal with a marked phenomenon in the process of legislation—the extent to which the Government consults at the preparatory stages of Bills and Statutory Instruments with interested and affected parties. Official and unofficial consultative procedures are now a widespread accompaniment to the legislative process, and the extent of the practice is explained by a deep-rooted belief in Britain that private parties should have opportunities of making their views known on decisions which affect them, and, especially, in the case of delegated legislation, by the need to make workable provisions in what are often very complex regulatory fields.

The preparatory stage of Bills and Statutory Instruments is now the main deliberative stage of legislation, carried on between Departments and interested groups. But the Cabinet, through its network of committees, has the decisive role in determining the final content, form and timing of legislative measures. Chapter V deals with the legislative structure of the Cabinet, and sets out the conventional relationships which have emerged between pressure groups, Departments and the Cabinet in the preparation of legislation.

Chapter VI deals with the Parliamentary stages of both primary and subordinate legislation. Although Parliament still spends more time discussing Bills and Statutory Instruments than in any other activity, legislation is not now effectively a Parliamentary function. Direct Parliamentary participation in legislation is restricted to attempts to engineer minor adjustments to the Government's plans, and the main purpose of the Parliamentary stages is to dissect and expose the Government's intentions and to clarify the consequences of them for the electorate. This is an important function of a representative assembly, the facilities for which could be considerably developed. The last chapter contains some discussion of recent proposals for Parliamentary reform which are directed towards this problem.

Inevitably, the coverage of a book as short as this has had to be restricted. There is nothing included on the annual financial legislation of the British Government. This, whilst showing some of the characteristics of the 'ordinary' legislative process, is bound by special Parliamentary procedural rules which can only be dealt with adequately in an extended survey. Fortunately this has recently been supplied by Professor Gordon Reid, in his book *The Politics of Financial Control*, which shows clearly that the processes of financial legislation in Britain are even more tightly controlled by the executive than is the case with ordinary public legislation. Nor is there anything directly on Private Members' legislation. In recent years this has illustrated some aspects of British politics in a fascinating way, but the ground rules are so different that it would require separate treatment if it were to be dealt with satisfactorily.

I

Legislation as a Process

THE end-products of legislation are easily recognized. They are Acts of Parliament as published in the *Statutes Revised*, and the contents of the collected annual volumes of Statutory Instruments.

Difficulties arise, however, when a conceptual definition of legislation is attempted—to try to show how, in substance, legislation differs from other broad governmental processes such as administration and adjudication. Attempts at a rigid classification along conceptual lines break down at the margins, and the conclusion cannot be avoided that the main differences between the ways in which determinations of public questions are made in any governmental system are largely procedural, and do not relate to any general inherent functional differences between the main activities of public authorities.

A conceptual definition of legislation which is often attempted states that it consists, to quote one authority, 'of the making of determinations which are issued to indicated but unnamed and unspecified persons or situations'.[1] Here the important characteristic of legislation is regarded as being that of generality of application. Another definition, substantially similar, and attempting to distinguish between legislation and the work of the courts, suggests that legislation normally 'affects the rights of individuals in the abstract and must be applied in a further proceeding before the legal position of an individual will be touched by it, whilst adjudication operates concretely upon individuals in their individual capacity'.[2] The Donoughmore-Scott Report on Ministers' Powers in 1932 similarly held that 'the power to issue a particular command' was 'in no sense legislative'.[3] Other attempts at defining a legislative function rely on the fact that legislation characteristically looks to the future, whilst judicial enquiries investigate present or past facts.

---

[1] K. C. Davis, *Administrative Law*, St Paul, 1951, p. 54.
[2] *Ibid.*
[3] *Report of the Committee on Ministers' Powers*, Cmd. 4060, 1932, p. 20.

Yet these definitions are all in some way lacking in precision. It is true that most acts of legislatures, if not all, establish rights and duties with respect either to the population generally or to classes of people or situations which are defined, sometimes closely, but not enumerated. But Private Acts enacted by Parliament, and Statutory Instruments promulgated by Government Departments, are often directed to the problems of a small identified group or an individual, and the generality of Public Acts of Parliament is always a matter of degree. Administrative agencies also make general directives and rules, through the medium of statutory or prerogative powers, through financial rulings, or by means of interpretations, announcements or circulars. Similarly the decisions of courts may involve innumerable parties or unnamed classes of the community. Again, although legislation usually looks to the future, it is occasionally retrospective in its effect whilst the judicial decisions with which it is usually contrasted in this respect, although normally based on past occurrences, also often attempt to prescribe future conduct.

It thus appears that precise definition of governmental functions in the abstract is not possible,[4] nor particularly desirable. The same activity may usefully be regarded as one thing or another depending on the particular context; such imprecision allows an empirical instead of an *a priori* assessment to be made of the appropriate procedures to be followed in making particular types of determination. Hence this short book will take as its opening proposition that what differentiates legislation from other broad governmental activities are the special procedures which are followed in developing and applying a legislative project, and to some extent the special personnel who are employed at some stages of the process. By concentrating attention on the procedures which are available to government for decision-making, this standpoint prevents analyses of governmental activity being made in terms of formal and misleading categories and doctrines—for example, the 'separation of powers' or the 'sovereignty of Parliament'. It permits a fresh look to be taken at some of the received doctrines of the constitution, and allows scope for empirical

---

[4] Attempts at a conceptual approach to governmental activities are bound to entail semantic difficulties. The search which has been made by many authorities for 'true' categories of legislative, judicial or administrative action has led to the common verbal error of assuming that definitions have an unchanging content which exhaust the characteristics of a particular type of activity. Neither the processes of definition nor of classification can make sense unless the context and purpose of the exercise is taken into account. The error as to the 'proper' meaning of words and as to 'true' definitions is still very widespread. For examples in this particular context see the *Report of the Committee on Ministers' Powers*, 1932, which is riddled with them.

proposals for reform of stages of the process to be freely advanced on their merits.

The modern legislative process in Britain is a multi-stage process, in which different criteria and constraints operate at each level. The governing procedures associated with the modern process are those of consultation by the executive with organized interest groups, followed by Parliamentary investigation of the general and special merits of the proposal. There is usually also a later 'administrative' stage, where Statutory Instruments are promulgated. This stage makes use of a number of developed procedures, of which consultation with affected parties and with expert advisory agencies is again the most marked, to specifically determine the general directions or declarations contained in parent statutes. All these stages, with their accompanying procedures, are now under the detailed direction of the political executive in Britain. Professor Griffith remarks that 'legislation today is more a Governmental than a Parliamentary function. Parliament has its part to play in this process but the extent to which this part should be played must be determined by reference to the characteristics and capabilities of the Parliamentary body',[5] and quotes John Stuart Mill in his support: 'While it is essential to representative government that the practical supremacy of the State should reside in the representatives of the people, it is an open question what actual functions, what precise part in the machinery of government, shall be directly and personally discharged by the representative body... In order to determine ..., what portions of the business of government the representative assembly should hold in its own hands, it is necessary to consider what kinds of business a numerous body is competent to perform properly'.[6]

This statement supports the general view that the extent of the participation of any agency in the legislative process should be largely determined by the contribution it can make through its characteristic mode of operation and the aptitudes of its personnel. The assertion is, however, probably too rational and too unpolitical to serve as a complete explanation of the degree of Parliament's involvement in the legislative process at various times. It does not, as will be seen below, provide a full rationale for the extent of delegated legislation in Britain at the present day. The very large number of Statutory Instruments which are annually made in Britain is only partly due to the unsuitability of Parliament to deal with certain types of legislative detail. A further explanation is that the Government

[5] J. A. G. Griffith, 'The Place of Parliament in the Legislative Process', *Modern Law Review*, Vol. 14, 1951, p. 291.

[6] John Stuart Mill, *Considerations on Representative Government*, Chapter V. Quoted in Griffith, *op. cit.*, p. 291.

usually has full political control of Parliament, and hence is able to retain as much legislative authority in its own hands as it thinks both necessary and convenient, and exercises its powers in this respect to the full.

Nor can purely functional considerations of the suitability of Parliament for certain tasks explain the legislative monopoly which Parliament insisted upon in periods earlier than that in which Mill wrote, when legislation was almost entirely a Parliamentary process. In the eighteenth and early nineteenth centuries Parliament stood in a loose constitutional relationship to a monarchical executive, which, except in a few traditional areas of public policy, like defence, foreign affairs and Customs and Excise, possessed little in the way of extensive administrative machinery or a trained civil service. With little or no conception of public policy outside these realms, the government did not regard itself as the natural initiator of legislation. Without extensive administrative reform, which Parliament was reluctant to see occur since it might add to the political power of the monarch, and in a period of relative social and political inertia, there was little possibility of social and economic reform by broad legislative action. Dicey wrote that 'From the beginning of the eighteenth century 'till pretty nearly the time of the Reform Bill, the chief duty of the Ministry was not the passing of laws, but the guidance of national policy. Chatham was the leading statesman of his time and country, but we cannot, it is said, attribute to him a single material amendment of the law'.[7] Or Lord Russell, speaking in 1841: 'If we look back to the greatest statesman which the country has ever produced—to those whose names are most regarded for the genius and ability which they displayed at the direction of affairs—if we look back to Sir R. Walpole, to Lord Chatham, to Mr Pitt and to Mr Fox—if we refer to the administrations of these great men, and then cast our eyes on the statute book, for the purpose of seeing what laws they have placed there, and what were the legislative measures they recommended and carried through Parliament, I fear that we shall meet with but a meagre return, indeed, for our labour. It is not, that those Ministers did not answer all that was required of them in their time—it is not that they were not fully equal to the conduct of affairs, according to the principles they professed—but that the usages of the constitution did not then require, that those at the head of the Government should bring forward legislative measures.'

Changes in the law were either brought about by the courts systematizing and extending the common law, or by private legislation. The Private Act of Parliament was the typical legislative vehicle of the eighteenth century and the first half of the nineteenth century,

[7] Quoted in Griffith, *op. cit.*, p. 283.

characteristic of an age which was still highly localized in its society and politics. Private Bill procedure gave the country enclosures of agricultural land, railways, docks and harbours, river improvements, water supplies, and many local authority services. 'It was the making of the Britain of the Industrial Revolution, and the foundation of our Victorian inheritance.' Great social and economic changes were brought about piecemeal by private legislation initiated by outside interests, and applying to particular areas, particular proprietors and particular authorities. It was not until the nineteenth century was well advanced that the central government attempted to take over the direction of these momentous changes and to regulate them by general enactments.

Private Bill legislation was a means of extending and adjusting, with safeguards to the public interest and compensation to private parties, the balance of rights and obligations within the community. Parliament's task was to adjudicate in the conflict, if any, between a proposal and the public interest, 'without unduly restricting private enterprise', as the historian of Private Bill legislation has dryly observed.[8] It developed for this purpose a distinctive judicial type of procedure, with little prior investigation of the subject-matter of the legislation by Parliament, and which was concerned mainly with the propositions, counter-propositions and supporting evidence which was put before Parliament by private parties.

Holdsworth, in his *History of English Law*, talks of 'the excessive individuality of the statutes passed by the Legislature in the eighteenth century', and adds 'Though such emergencies as the rebellion of 1745 might lead to important domestic legislation initiated by the government, for the most part the initiation of legislation was left to individual peers or members of the House of Commons'.[9] Maitland, the constitutional historian and lawyer, calls the eighteenth century 'the age of privilegia. It seems afraid to rise to the dignity of a general proposition. . . . We may attribute this to jealousy of the Crown'.[10] Certainly Private Bill legislation was a device which Parliament could use for minimizing the powers of what was, for a considerable part of this period, an unreformed and privileged monarchical bureaucracy, and substituting for it Parliamentary control over the grant of powers to corporations, local authorities and local justices. These were enforced not by a central civil service in the hands of governments which Parliament mistrusted and could not completely control, but by a judiciary which was independent of the

---

[8] Frederick Clifford, *A History of Private Bill Legislation*, London, 1887, Vol. 1.

[9] Sir William Holdsworth, *A History of English Law*, Vol. IX, p. 371. Quoted in Griffith, *op. cit.*, p. 283.

[10] F. W. Maitland, *The Constitutional History of England*, pp. 383–4.

Crown and a natural ally of Parliament in attempts to restrain executive authority. Yet it is doubtful whether this factor is sufficient in itself to explain the immense amount of eighteenth- and early nineteenth-century private legislation. Procedure by Private Bill was natural to a society which wished to make marginal adjustments to the reigning state of affairs, but which could not conceive of consciously-directed broad social and economic reform.

A change can be discerned after the 1832 Reform Act, and after the extensive civil service reforms of the period 1780-1830, with the consequent decline in the eighteenth-century system of monarchical government by influence and patronage. Maitland, in the passage cited above, continues 'The change is a gradual one ... Parliament begins to *legislate* with considerable vigour, to overhaul the whole law of the country ... but about the same time it gives up the attempt to *govern* the country, to say what commons shall be enclosed, what roads shall be widened, what boroughs shall have paid constables and so forth. It begins to lay down general rules about these matters and to entrust their working partly to officials, to secretaries of state, to boards of commissioners, who for this purpose are endowed with new statutory powers, partly to the law courts'.[11] In 1901, Sir Courtney Ilbert, a great nineteenth-century Parliamentary Counsel to the Treasury, wrote 'The shifting of the centre of political gravity after the Reform Act of 1832, the enormous strides of scientific discovery, commercial enterprise, and industrial activity, the new problems presented by the massing of great numbers in towns and factories under artificial conditions, the awakened interest in the moral, mental and material welfare of the working classes, involving demands for enlargement of the functions both of the central and of the local government—all these causes have materially altered the character and increased the volume of Victorian legislation ... the net result of the legislative activity which has characterized, though with different degrees of intensity, the period since 1832, has been the building up piecemeal of an administrative machine of great complexity.... The legislation required for this purpose is enough, and more than enough, to absorb the whole legislative time of the House of Commons and the problem of finding the requisite time for this class of legislation increases in difficulty every year...'[12]

With the growth of administrative machinery, the rise of national political parties and the centralization of political responsibility in the Cabinet, came the gradual acceptance by the government of responsibilty for presenting a legislative programme to Parliament, adumbrated before elections by the request for a mandate of sorts.

[11] *Ibid.*
[12] Sir Courtney Ilbert, *Legislative Methods and Forms*, Oxford, 1901, pp. 212-13.

This process was virtually complete by the 1860s, the highwater mark of Victorian Liberalism. Liberalism as an ideology implied a distinctive view of the British constitution. It was a theory of popular representation, of government by consent, and of the accountability of government to Parliament. As one commentator has described it, Liberalism on these terms was a theory of legitimate power, and power was to be used along reformist lines. For this purpose Liberal governments turned to the legislative device of the Public General Act of Parliament, which became the 'perfect instrument' of a Liberal capitalist society. The Reform Act of 1832, treating all £10 house-holders as equal, and using state power to reform the electoral system whilst offering no compensation for the loss of political rights, was a great triumph of the Public General Act.[13] Through the period of legislative Utilitarianism—Benthamism—to the middle and later years of what Dicey called the nineteenth-century age of collectivism, the vehicle of the Public General Act was used to create, firstly, the statutory framework within which Liberal capitalism could develop, and then the great reforms which ameliorated the worst of the evils of the industrial revolution.

The relationship of government and Parliament in this process was one of partnership. Legislative procedure in Parliament was radically simplified between 1830 and 1880, to facilitate the scrutiny and criticism of governmental programmes of legislation, and to assist in the sifting of information and the determination of facts which was an essential feature of the deliberative stage of the legislative process. Parliamentary procedural development in the nineteenth century was a long and complex process, whereby a traditionally 'obstructive' procedure, dating in its major forms from the seventeenth-century conflicts between Parliament and the Stuart monarchs, was transformed into a procedure which facilitated constructive criticism of the financial and legislative proposals of politically responsible governments, whilst severely restricting the opportunities of Private Members to bring in legislation. The assumption behind the new legislative procedure was that Parliament as a representative body was competent to dispose of all matters coming before it without according any procedural formalities to the interests who were affected by particular measures. The Parliamentary procedure which was evolved to control legislative proceedings was designed to secure fair discussion, adequate deliberation and general efficiency in the disposition of legislative matters coming before it, without giving consultative rights to outside individuals or groups. On the other hand, mid-Victorian Parliaments did not relinquish all initiative to the government in the

[13] See C. Hughes, *The British Statute Book*, London, 1957, p. 45.

formulation and preparation of legislative projects. An elaborate machinery of Select Committees, unrestricted in procedure and with wide-ranging powers to acquaint Parliamentarians with points of view in the community was employed specially to inform the House of Commons concerning particular matters with which they had to deal.

Victorian legislation, enacted in massive Public General Acts, dealt often with primary and elementary social and economic relationships. As such, it was right that it should engage almost the entire attention of an increasingly representative Parliament, often in the preparation of Bills, always in the shaping of their detail. With the exception of some technical industrial legislation, most of the subjects of nineteenth-century statutes did not call for much specialized knowledge and were well within the competence of the Parliamentarians of that epoch. Legal, social and economic relationships and their interaction with government policy are now immeasurably more complex, however, and the roles of government much more subtle, technical and sophisticated. Modern Statutory Instruments, drawn up by Government Departments under powers conferred by enabling legislation, and the procedures which have been developed to aid this type of legislation, can match these conditions of complexity and subtlety. They can bring to bear on the problems which are raised by governmental intervention at all points of the life of the community the collective knowledge and experience of highly skilled and organized social and economic groups, and expert Departmental advisers.

Yet although there have been many encomiums on the Public General Act as a legislative device, there has been a curious reluctance to recognize the legitimacy and permanence of Departmental legislation as the main twentieth-century vehicle of legislative regulation. Partly because the Public General Act was identified with the 'rule of law' (although much that has been done by its agency would not have met with Dicey's approval), and, to the same extent, supported formal-legal concepts of the legislative sovereignty of Parliament, it has been regarded as the normal end-product of the legislative process, from which Ministerial legislation is a distinctly inferior, temporary derogation, suspected by right-wing lawyers, at least, of containing the seeds of the overthrow of responsible government in Britain.[14] Yet the practice is by no means new, although the

---

[14] For example, a chapter in G. W. Keeton's *The Passing of Parliament* is headed 'The Menace of Delegated Legislation', and the more measured study of administrative law by Sir C. K. Allen is still entitled *Law and Orders*, a punning opposition of terms which leaves little doubt concerning the author's view of the status of subordinate legislation.

present huge volume of Departmental legislation is mainly a post-1945 phenomenon. A number of Victorian statutes delegated law-making powers to public authorities. Most statutes of a regulatory type, usually Public Health and Factory Acts, contained wide enabling clauses.[15] The main impetus to Departmental legislation, however, was given in this century by two world wars, when very wide public control of employment, production and the economy generally was instituted. After 1945 the growth of the Welfare State and the managed economy also greatly extended the areas of government contact with national life.

Yet despite the rapid growth in the volume of subordinate legislation and its importance in the regulatory roles of government, official enquiries into the place of statutory powers to make regulations in the legislative process have never directly recognized their potential. Instead the investigations have been almost entirely negatively conceived, concerned mainly with confining the scope of the process and improving judicial and Parliamentary controls over it. This was particularly true of the 1932 Committee on Ministers' Powers, whose attempts at a formal and outdated analysis of governmental processes led it into semantic confusion, which together with its suspicious approach to the subject-matter of the enquiry, set the pattern for much subsequent discussion of delegated legislation.[16] The only other official enquiry into the scope and procedures of delegated legislation has been the Davies Committee—a Select Committee of the House of Commons—which brought in a narrower and more legalistic Report in 1953.[17]

[15] For examples, see Sir W. Holdsworth, *A History of English Law*, edited by A. L. Goodhart and H. G. Hanbury, London, 1964, Vol. XIV, pp. 100–3.

[16] It is significant of the way in which the Committee approached its task that Miss Ellen Wilkinson, a member of the Committee, was moved to add a personal disclaimer to the tone of its Report, and was supported in this by another member Professor Laski. Miss Wilkinson thought the Report 'gave the impression that the delegating of legislation is a necessary evil, inevitable in the present state of pressure on Parliamentary time, but nevertheless a tendency to be watched with misgiving and carefully safeguarded. I feel that in the conditions of the modern state, which not only has to undertake immense new social services, but which before long may be responsible for the greater part of the industrial and commercial activities of the country, the practice of Parliament delegating legislation and the power to make regulations, instead of being grudgingly conceded, ought to be widely extended, and new ways devised to facilitate the process.' (*Report of the Committee on Ministers' Powers*, Cmd. 4060, 1932, Annex VI.)

Whilst noting the special political pleading, this passage is evidence of justifiable irritation with a state of mind which, so far as subordinate legislation and Ministers' powers generally are concerned, persistently interprets the modern British constitution in terms of a series of temporary exceptions and divergences from a mid-Victorian constitutional ideal.

[17] *Report of the Select Committee on Delegated Legislation*, H.C. 310-1, 1953.

B

Much of the suspicion of delegated legislation is aroused by the fact that civil servants are intimately associated with its procedures, and that the opportunities for participation in the process by representative and politically responsible members of the House of Commons are necessarily limited. The popular criticisms of the civil service were summed up by the Committee on the Training of Civil Servants: 'While the defects commonly attributed to it are not the monopoly of the Civil Service, it may be that the conditions of the public service tend to foster particular weaknesses ... the faults most commonly enumerated are over-devotion to precedent, remoteness from the rest of the community, inaccessibility and faulty handling of the general public, lack of initiative, etc.'. It may be that the civil service, with its ability to evade immediate political responsibility, is unfitted to carry the sole weight of public policies which are matters of political dispute, or which are likely to bear very heavily on sections of the public. But charges of remoteness from some sections of public opinion and of inaccessibility must give way when the extent of consultation by the civil service with organized groups and its ability to have recourse to a vast network of advisory committees is taken into account.

As a result, whilst legislative procedure in Parliament has been relatively static for some time, the Departmental phase of the modern legislative process has seen considerable technical advances, which have had the result of introducing a marked degree of procedural flexibility and sensitivity into legislative rule-making by administrative agencies. Of these, the most widespread and influential procedure is the informal consultation with interests in the making of subordinate legislation. As Professor Griffith has remarked of consultative procedures in this sphere, 'When this practice works well and fully, it solves much of the constitutional problem involved in the delegation of legislative power. For to Parliament—a general body—are left those general matters for the examination of which it is both fit and has opportunity, while to the interests affected or their representatives is left the examination of particular, specialized and technical details'.[18] The subject of consultation in the making of Statutory Instruments will be taken up more fully later,[19] but it is worth while noting here other more formal statutory procedures which have been developed as a part of the process of subordinate law-making.

Firstly there is the procedure by individual objection, whereby persons affected by a proposed Statutory Instrument have the

[18] J. A. G Griffith, 'Delegated Legislation—Some Recent Developments', *Modern Law Review*, Vol. 12, 1949, p. 306.
[19] See Chapter IV.

opportunity of stating a case to the responsible authority. Most nine-teenth- and twentieth-century Factory Acts made this sort of provision for individual objection followed by a public enquiry.[20] A more modern example of this type of statutory requirement is con-tained in the Radioactive Substances Act of 1948, which provides for the Ministerial proposal to make regulations to be published, with opportunity for objections to be followed by either a public enquiry or a personal hearing. This Departmental procedure is similar to the general procedure which was required by the Rules Publication Act of 1893, an early statutory attempt to control the process of subordinate legislation by making consultation with affected in-terests compulsory. The Act, unfortunately defective in many ways, required the draft regulations to be published at least forty days before they were to be made, and required the Department con-cerned to consider any representations made by any public body. The Statutory Instruments Act of 1946, which repealed and replaced the Rules Publication Act, did not provide for general preliminary notice and objection. The Lord Chancellor explained that Depart-mental practice had overtaken this statutory provision: 'We no longer promulgate the regulations or rules in the Gazette and wait for representations to be made. We go to the trade or interest concerned and deal with it by getting them round the table, hearing what they have to say and then drafting the rules after obtaining their views.'[21]

Some parent statutes require a Department to consult with speci-fied interests before making a Statutory Instrument, usually with local authorities, statutory advisory bodies, or representatives of affected parties. Numerous Acts of Parliament specify this type of procedure,[22] and hence formally require what in any case appears to be Departmental practice. A much more formal procedure is where the subordinate legislation has positively to be approved by a statutory body, acting as a type of specialized 'sub-Parliament' for this purpose. The effect of these statutory provisions, as Griffith has pointed out, 'is that the Minister must either accept the report [of the committee] with its proposed amendments or be prepared to defend his refusal to do so in Parliament. It is right that the last word should rest with the Minister; but he will be a very foolish Minister who repeatedly insists on having it by refusing to accept the advice of a statutory body specially charged with advising him'.[23]

The most important parent statute to contain this provision, in

---

[20] See Griffith, *op. cit.*, p. 308.
[21] 139 *H. L. Debs*, 5s. col. 330.
[22] For examples, see Griffith, *op. cit.*, p. 310.
[23] *Op. cit.*, p. 311.

terms of the number of individuals who are affected by regulations made under it, is the National Insurance Act of 1946. The Act creates a National Insurance Advisory Committee, whose task it is to embody the interests in national insurance of innumerable classes and sections of the population. It consists of members appointed after consultation with employers' and workers' organizations and friendly societies, and has provision for the appointment of other members drawn from public life. Very close liaison has been established between the Ministry and the Advisory Committee, and the high quality of National Insurance administration owes much to the Committee's work.

Finally there should be noted those cases where subordinate legislation is actually prepared by the affected interests. Here the power to draft a Statutory Instrument is delegated to an individual or group, and the Minister becomes the confirming authority. There are many variations on this procedure, and participation in the legislative process by the interests concerned can go no farther than this.

In sum, if private legislation was a product of an age which had little concept of public policy, or of national politics, the Public General Act of Parliament was the typical legislative vehicle of reformist governments, articulated and resolved by new Parliamentary processes. The Statutory Instrument, however, is the product of a period when political power is more dispersed, when there is a greater amount of agreement on basic state policy than ever before, and when the weight of discussion and political argument has been thrown into the area of administrative adjustment.

The legislative process in Britain is now complex: it comprises deliberative, Parliamentary and administrative stages, over all of which executive political influence is predominant. Legislation is now an almost exclusively executive function, modified, sometimes heavily, by practices of group and Parliamentary consultation. As a result of this large measure of centralized political control of the process, it is possible in Britain for the executive to bring in scientifically planned programmes of legislative change, and to establish reasoned legislative priorities. On the other hand, the process is not one which occurs entirely along a chain of command and assent; powerful group pressures are exerted at all its stages, from the preparation of legislative projects, throughout the processes of scrutiny and criticism, and bear particularly heavily on the administrative stage when legislation is put into operation. The process of legislation could equally well be termed a continuous process of consultation, reconciling group and party interests to its objects, and acting as a powerful legitimating and integrating influence within the constitution.

II

The Sources of Legislative Policy

IN his book *Congressional Government*, Woodrow Wilson said of the origins of legislative policy: '[Legislation] is an aggregate, not a simple production. It is impossible to tell how many persons, opinions and influences have entered into its composition'. Another American observer, S. K. Bailey, after an analysis of one Act of the US Congress, concluded: 'One generalization is that the process is almost unbelievably complex. Legislative policy-making appears to be the result of a confluence of factors streaming from an almost endless number of tributaries: national experience, the contributions of social theorists, the clash of powerful economic interests, the quality of Presidential leadership, other institutional and personal ambitions and administrative arrangements in the Executive Branch, the initiative, effort and ambitions of individual legislators and their governmental and non-governmental staffs, the policy commitments of political parties, and the predominant culture symbols in the minds of both leaders and followers in Congress'.[1] With appropriate substitutions, and with some changes of emphasis due to different constitutional situations, the description holds good for legislative policy-making in Britain.

Bagehot, in his *English Constitution*, described the English system of government as simple, with ultimate authority concentrated in the hands of the Cabinet, whose members were at the same time the efficient executive, and the leaders of both Parliament and the dominant political party. Although, a century later, the formal institutions of British government still present, in Bagehot's sense, the same 'simple' appearance, once their façade has been breached it is seen that the power wielded by them is not ultimate, but is in fact widely shared between official and unofficial agencies. A better description of the modern British system is Richard Rose's term 'composite government', by which is meant that political power is widely distributed amongst formal and informal institutions. On

[1] S. K. Bailey, *Congress makes a Law*, New York, 1950, p. 236.

the one hand, close examination shows that the formal institutions of British government are not as monolithic and hierarchical in their structure as is usually supposed. Ministers are faced with powerful and experienced civil service advisers and advisory structures, whose status and permanency within the Departmental system are sources of authority in their dealings with transient and usually amateur political heads of Departments. Ministers are also constrained by pressures institutionalized in powerful inter-Departmental advisory committees and cabinet agencies. On the other hand, the formal policy processes of British government are not carried out in a vacuum. The Departmental structure is increasingly characterized by an agency-clientele relationship with powerful organized interests; Departments are usually wise to take note of the attitudes of these pressure groups, whose adherence to official policy is often vital to its success. 'The processes of policy are plural; in effect, government is a composite of political and social institutions'.[2]

The legislative policy of any one government is derived from a variety of sources. Traditionally, the formal device of the electoral mandate has been taken to explain the sources of policy. Mandates, however, are often too vague for precise realization, and in any case empirical studies of legislative programmes do not confirm this explanation. As Eckstein has remarked, 'In an average session legislation for which a mandate has been given occupies only a fraction of the time spent on Bills'.[3] He draws from this the characteristic conclusion that the British government owes its privilege of enjoying almost a monopoly of introducing legislative projects firstly, because of a wide national belief that it is the business of a British government to govern, and secondly, to the political discipline which it is able to exert over Parliament, rather than as a result of the sanction given by the democratic nature of a mandate won by a party at the polls.

One of the earliest attempts to analyze the origins of British legislative policy, and the one on which Eckstein bases his conclusions, was made by Sir Ivor Jennings in his classic study of Parliament, the first edition of which appeared in 1937. Jennings takes the legislative programme which was achieved in the 1936-37 session of Parliament and analyzes each Act in terms of the dominant influence on its origin. Of Acts which reached the statute book, nine were wholly political in origin, and were dependent primarily on Cabinet policy decisions; twenty-seven were comparatively non-controversial Departmental measures of varying importance; nine resulted largely from pressure group demand; three could be attributed to governmental policy highly modified by outside pressure; seven could be attributed

[2] Richard Rose, *Politics in England*, London, 1965, p. 213.
[3] In Beer and Ulam (ed.) *Patterns of Government*, 2nd ed., N.Y. 1965, p. 133.

to Departmental policy similarly modified; two were derived from local government associations and two originated with private Members of Parliament.[4] This, however, referred to the first year of a new Parliament, in which policy measures would figure more heavily than in the later stages of a Government's tenure. With Governments newly in office, the source of major legislative projects will be the party programme, which commits the Government to early legislative action in a variety of spheres. Later in a Parliament this source will not be so important. For example, in a review of pending legislation made by *The Times* in October, 1962 only one measure, facilitating shareholding by small investors, was mentioned as originating in the Conservative Party's 1959 election manifesto. In a similar review of pending legislation for the 1963-64 session, which listed twenty-two Bills, sixteen could be regarded as primarily Departmental in origin, eight of them resting to a major extent on the reports of Departmental committees. In two instances pressure groups were mentioned as important influences without formal committees having been set up. In five cases local government bodies or other non-central government agencies had been influential in the proposed legislation. Four Bills dealt with, and had been discussed with, Commonwealth and foreign countries. There was no measure which stemmed from an electoral programme.[5]

The foregoing illustrates the fact that not only does public legislative policy emerge in a number of ways, and in different types of legislative decision, but also that most legislative projects derive from Departmental experience. Much of the legislation which the Cabinet is willing to sponsor comes from the permanent staffs of the Departments, whose wide experience and detailed contacts with organized groups make them sensitive to needed reforms. Legislative decisions of this type are often an extension of Departmental administration, and serve to clarify or strengthen existing administrative or financial authority by legislative means. They can arise either as a result of Departmental administrative experience, or from the pressures of the group or groups which are intimately connected with the Department's area of responsibility—most typically, from a combination of both factors. However, the Cabinet does not operate simply to put through Parliament the legislation which is proposed by Departmental civil servants. With some Departmental projects the Cabinet in power has no sympathy, or is actively opposed to them. Adoption of the policy has to await more favourable circumstances.

[4] Sir Ivor Jennings, *Parliament*, (3rd ed.) Appendix 2.
[5] See *The Times*, September 19, 1963, 'Many Bills Compete for Priority in Next Parliamentary Session', and Richard Rose, *op. cit.*, p. 213.

There are legislative decisions of a second type, when a Government decides either to reverse a long-standing policy or to enter a new area of activity. These decisions involve apparently sharp discontinuities with past practice. Often, however, the two types of legislative decision cannot be sharply differentiated. It is seldom, for example, that a new legislative departure cannot build on existing administrative knowledge and experience, and often a 'new' decision is a synthesis of existing policies.

Two major factors affect the development of legislative policy in Britain. The first is the fragmentation and dispersal of political forces that has already been noticed as a marked characteristic of the British political system. It reflects the division of the electorate into a wide and complex spectrum of economic, social and occupational groups. As Sir C. K. Allen has remarked, 'the elements which contribute to the framing of modern legislation are numerous and diverse. They are bound to be so in crowded communities where public opinion is not one collective and unanimous sentiment, but is fragmented among many different sections and interests'.[6] In its relation to the British political party system, this fragmentation of political power manifests itself in the attempt by the major parties to link themselves through their programmes with the largest possible number of producer and consumer groups within the community. S. H. Beer characterizes the post-war period in British political life as one of pluralist politics, in the sense of the existence of a multiplicity of fairly autonomous centres of economic and political power, linked with the major parties at many points, and in response to whose demands a great deal of policy is made.[7] This does not mean that there are no differences between the major British political parties, either in point of their sources of support or their policies; the extent and nature of the links between pressure groups and parties is to some extent modified by party policy, 'by distinct party conceptions of the common good' which each holds. But on the other hand the electoral competition between the parties which has been a marked feature of British politics since 1945 and the consequent need to gain the widest support amongst the electorate has led to considerable overlap both in sources of party support and in party programmes.

Pressure groups, during elections, attempt to commit parties to particular policies. Once a government is elected, the struggle is transferred to Whitehall, and, to a lesser extent, Westminster. The formal institutional counterpart to the scattered sources of political power are the large central government Departments, each responsible for public policy in distinct areas, and each with its separate clientele of

---

⁶ Sir C. K. Allen, *Law in the Making*, Oxford, 1958, p. 418.

⁷ S. H. Beer, *Modern British Politics*, London, 1965, Chapters XI and XII.

pressure groups in the electorate. A less important institutional counterpart to the dispersal of political force within the community arises from the identification of Parliamentary party committees of MPs or inter-party groups of MPs with the same outside factions. The Departments, the Parliamentary backbench groups and pressure groups are drawn together both formally and informally in the legislative process, creating centres of activity engaged constantly in particular areas of public policy, and ideas for legislative projects emerge from these interactions.

In general, the continuity and stability of these attachments of groups, Departments and Parliamentarians means that legislative policy is fairly easily and smoothly made. The attachments also explain the high degree of continuity evident in British legislation, since Departments have a large sphere of latitude in determining their domestic policies. This fragmentation of political power, and of the centres of policy making, is however, offset by a number of integrating and co-ordinating elements in the machinery of British government. Whilst no Cabinet or Prime Minister is so completely in charge of the policy-making processes as to be able to present a completely planned and integrated legislative programme for Parliamentary consideration, Departments of State are subject to some extent to the co-ordinating control of inter-Departmental advisory structures, and to continuous Treasury control over the cost of their projects. They are also responsible in policy matters to powerful Cabinet committees, which bring together the interests of many Ministers in the legislative policy of Departments. Similarly backbench groups of MPs are subject in their relations with pressure groups to the constraints imposed on them by the need for party unity.

In addition to the dispersal of political power in the community, another important contributory factor in the making of legislative policy is technical specialization. This factor tends to focus interest less on political pressures and more on facts and technical non-political assessments of public problems. This is a growing accompaniment to modern legislation and administration. The use of specialist personnel in Government Departments, the constant use by Departments of expert technical advisory committees, the recent foundation in a number of Departments of research units, and the work of independent research organizations, affect legislative policy in a variety of direct and indirect ways. These executive developments have been paralleled in Parliament by the recent concentration on investigatory and technical devices such as specialist Select Committees, the use of technical assessors by Parliamentary bodies, and the development of a specialist legislative reference service in the House of Commons. This factor is particularly important in its bearing on delegated legislation. Policy at the level of primary legislation is seldom so overwhelmingly technical for there to be no general opinion about it at all, but a great deal of subordinate legislation seldom has interest for any except a very limited class of the electorate, or for technical practitioners. The nature of the government's tasks and problems have changed greatly since the nineteenth-century heyday of the generalist administrator and amateur MP. The problems of management and planning entailed in 'positive government' call for different, and more specialized skills. The relationship between technical and political expertize in Departments has yet to be fully worked out; what is certain is that specialists will continue to take on greater responsibility in policy-making in most fields of modern government.

Leadership in policy adoption in Britain is fairly clear-cut and straightforward. With Departmental legislative policy it rests in the first place with the Departmental Minister, whose support and involvement is needed if a policy is to be taken up and made politically live. The relationship between Minister and his permanent Departmental advisers is now not as clear as the constitutional doctrines would have it, but the conventions concerning Ministerial responsibility and the anonymity of the Civil Service still require that a Department or Departmental Division must convince the political head of the Department of the need for and the viability of a particular legislative project if the process of publicity and political support for it is to be put in hand. On the other hand, whilst they are powerful as leaders in policy adoption, Ministers are not unconstrained in their role as brokers of Departmental policy. Their function is to be aware of the political dimensions of policy and in this their relationships with their backbench Parliamentary supporters and with the Cabinet are highly important.

The Prime Minister performs the greatest single role in policy adoption in the British system; his leadership of party and of the Cabinet secure this, although the highly political nature of the office means that his role is often more noticeable in the run-up to an election than in the making of legislative policy during the lifetime of a government. His role is also more marked in the case of controversial legislation than in the majority of Departmental projects. The extent to which the political leadership of the Prime Minister is accepted, the expectations of strong government on the part of Parliament and electorate alike, the high degree of political discipline and cohesion amongst the government's political supporters, make it possible for major legislative changes to be accomplished in Britain with a smaller degree of national consensus than is needed in most other developed political systems. Nonetheless, wide agreement is sought, even though it is not necessary; consultative procedures are used to bring affected interests into the stages of formulation of legislative projects, and attempts are usually made to gain the widest possible consent to legislative policy. No government, however strong and firmly established, wishes for mere conformity with its policies. It also seeks to justify its proposals both inside and outside Parliament, and to convince Parliament and the affected groups of the electorate of its rightness. The sensitive liaison arrangements which all governments maintain with organized groups and with their own political supporters are important instruments in ensuring the relatively smooth operation of the legislative process.

It is very seldom that leadership in policy adoption is exercised by groups of MPs or by individual legislators in Parliament, except in comparatively minor areas of public policy, which can be dealt with by Private Members' Bills. Even here, the Cabinet, by making its assent to this type of legislation indispensable, exercises leadership in a negative fashion.

In conclusion, it can be seen how difficult it is to generalize about the sources of legislative policy. Any measure of real importance probably owes something to all the forces mentioned. Into it will have gone the pressures, of support, modification or opposition, of the groups in society which are affected by it. Into it will also have gone the personal contributions of a Minister and his Departmental advisers. The backgrounds and attitudes of Members of Parliament will normally have played some part, and the specialized knowledge of technical agencies of government will have been brought into play at some stage.

In so far as there are any uniformities in the provenance of legislation, a fairly typical recent example of a legislative measure of major importance was the Resale Prices Bill, which was introduced into Parliament in February, 1964, by Mr Edward Heath, the then President of the Board of Trade and Secretary of State for Industry, Trade and Regional Development. The Bill demonstrates clearly the multiplicity of influences which bear on legislative policy, and also the admixture of administrative experience, technical appraisal and political and social philosophy which enter, in some proportion, into all legislative projects. Most of all, it demonstrates the importance of the development of Departmental experience and attitudes, and shows quite clearly the indispensable role of the Minister in the process of policy adoption. Resale price maintenance has a long history in Britain as a trading policy, and the 1964 Bill constituted a considerable reversal of long-standing official attitudes towards it. The origins of price maintenance are to be found towards the end of the nineteenth century, in a reaction by manufacturers and some traders against the price-cutting of consumer goods by retailers. It is a policy by which the supplier of goods stipulates and enforces the price at which a product may be sold, and as such, was intimately bound up with the practice of manufacturer branding and national advertizing. As resale price maintenance became widespread, so too did the use of trade associations for the collective enforcement of RPM agreements on behalf of a number of manufacturers. In many cases the trade associations set up private enforcement systems to deal with retailers who cut prices below the recommended level, operating the sanction of withholding of supplies from proved offenders. Despite numerous court cases in which the legality of the enforcement system was called into question, RPM flourished. Official committees of enquiry into the practice were set up, directly or indirectly involving the Board of Trade, after the 1914-18 war, and during the inter-war depression period, but it was not until the Lloyd Jacob Committee Report of 1949 that resale price maintenance received its first major setback at the hands of the Government.

This Committee of enquiry was set up as part of the post-war Labour Government's campaign against monopoly and restrictive practices, and marks the beginning of the modern involvement of the Board of Trade with RPM. The Lloyd Jacob Committee's main recommendation was that the practice of collective resale price maintenance, i.e. the practice whereby each manufacturer's attempts to regulate the resale prices of his products were backed by the threat of withholding from price-cutting retailers the brands of all the manufacturers of similar products—should be abolished. The Lloyd Jacob Committee recommended, however, that any manufacturer should be allowed to prescribe and enforce resale prices for goods bearing his brand, if this were possible without resorting to collective boycott.

However, the Labour Government was prepared to go farther than this in abolishing the practice, and a White Paper issued by the Board of Trade in 1951 foreshadowed early legislation to make all forms of RPM other than the fixing of maximum prices illegal. From this date the Departmental policy of the Board of Trade appears to have been firmly fixed in the direction of total abolition. However, the electoral reverse of 1951 put Labour out of office, and legislation on any aspect of RPM was not introduced until 1956.

It was the reports of the Monopolies and Restrictive Practices Commission, the product of the same onslaught against monopoly which had produced the Lloyd Jacob Committee, which were instrumental in preparing the ground for the Restrictive Trade Practices Act of 1956. This Act had the effect, not of outlawing resale price maintenance as such, but of preventing the practice of collective

enforcement through trade associations. It shifted the means of pre-
serving the trading policy to individual manufacturers operating
singly. The total area of resale price maintenance was somewhat
diminished by the 1956 Act, and in the grocery trade it broke down
completely. On the other hand, a result of the legislation was to give
advantages to larger firms in promoting and enforcing individual
price maintenance in their products.

From 1956 onwards, opposition mounted to the practice of individual price maintenance. Although there was no direct enquiry into
the practice, either by Royal Commission or Departmental Committee, until 1960, a number of official reports of the technical
economic agencies of government touched on the practice in a highly
critical fashion. In the words of one commentator, after 1956 'the
attack on RPM became insistent'.[8] The short-lived Council on Prices,
Productivity and Incomes (the Cohen Commission) in its first
Report in 1958 commented that in the light of the emphasis which
the Conservative Government was placing on keeping prices low,
resale price maintenance ought to be 'carefully considered'. Its
second Report concluded, after an examination of price maintenance
in practice, that it 'undoubtedly operates to inhibit price reductions',
and that consideration of RPM in the particular context of preventing
general price inflation was not given much weight at the time that the
[1956] legislation was passed'. Similarly the Departmental Moloney
Committee on Consumer Protection took the unusual step in 1960
of asking for a directive from the Board of Trade as to whether RPM
fell within its terms of reference, and was obviously anxious to investigate its effect. By this time, however, the Board of Trade itself was
again active, and the Moloney Committee was told that a Departmental fact-finding enquiry was to be set up on the subject. The
Moloney Commission nevertheless reported that 'a few of our members considered that the existing law in favour of RPM was *prima
facie* inimical to the interest of the consumer'. Two further timely
and telling reports from a powerful technical agency were those in
1963 of the Monopolies Commission on motor accessories and wall-
paper. The reports were detailed, and their findings received wide
publicity. Both where quite unequivocal in their condemnation of
RPM as it operated in these two areas. Also in 1963 the Government-
sponsored Consumer Council recommended that resale price maintenance be made illegal, whilst in early 1964 the National Economic
Development Council also noted favourably the developments in the
Board of Trade to deal with the practice.

Hence by the early 1960s a wide spectrum of reputable and independent technical sources had appraised the economic effects of

[8] J. F. Pickering, *Resale Price Maintenance in Practice*, London, 1966, p. 216.

RPM and had produced reports which condemned either the general practice of price maintenance or individual instances of its operation. None of the sources were political, however, and none were in close relationship or necessarily influential with the Conservative Government. Similarly, although in the same period there can also be discerned something akin to a loose and unorganised anti-RPM lobby, consisting of academic economists, and multiple store and supermarket organizations who stood to gain from the abolition of price maintenance, its political strength was slight, as was that of the anti-RPM press. All these pressures were weak and diffuse, and cannot be considered a primary source of the 1964 Resale Prices Bill.

There was, officially, at least, no positive government policy towards individually maintained prices before 1963. The previous General Election was that of 1959, and the attitude of the Conservative Party at that election, to a very large extent determined by the links which the party had with the small shopkeepers, had been merely to maintain the existing arrangements that were being worked out under the 1956 legislation. This position was strongly underlined by numerous Conservative speakers during the 1959 campaign. In such a situation, without an official party line, and with the pressure against RPM diffuse, the attitude of the Board of Trade itself assumed considerable importance. If any one major source of the 1964 Bill can be discerned it lies in the matured policy of this Department. Officials of the Board of Trade had a long experience with RPM, dating back to the Profiteering Acts of the post-1918 period, and it would seem that there existed a historic Departmental policy of antagonism to the practice. This was given fresh impetus by the results of the 1960 fact-finding enquiry, which, it was widely believed, recommended the almost total prohibition of RPM. The report was neither published nor communicated privately to backbenchers, possibly because of the hostility of the Conservative Cabinet to its findings. When the enquiry was completed, in 1961, Macmillan's Cabinet contained at least two key members who were well-disposed towards price maintenance as a trading practice—R. A. Butler and Harold Macmillan himself, whose history as a successful publisher may have been as influential in determining his attitude as the political difficulties which would inevitably attend legislation to abolish RPM. It would appear that during Macmillan's premiership Cabinet opinion remained hostile to moves designed to ban price maintenance, and the Board of Trade could make no further progress. According to the *Financial Times*, the report of the Departmental fact-finding enquiry was brought to the Cabinet twice in this period by successive Presidents of the Board of Trade—Maudling and Erroll—but with no success.

Leadership in policy adoption in this case was ultimately exercised by the next President of the Board of Trade, Edward Heath. Heath took office in 1963 as the new Secretary of State for Industry, Trade and Regional Development in the reshuffle of Ministers consequent on Macmillan's resignation as Prime Minister. Heath's personal Conservative philosophy favoured the abolition of price maintenance. He had entered Parliament as a 'new' Conservative in 1950, when anti-monopoly feeling, the result of recent widespread nationalization, was at its height in the party. There is little doubt that his personal view favoured the lowering of the 'consumption barriers' amongst the electorate as a means of attaching consumers to Conservatism. The abolition of RPM was as much a policy of this type to Heath as were reduced restrictions on hire purchase, easier mortgages, and the encouragement of stock ownership by small investors, all designed to produce a Conservative-oriented property-owning democracy. Moreover, Heath's previous governmental experience had convinced him of the need to abolish price maintenance. He had previously been concerned with the negotiations to secure British entry into the Common Market, when resale price maintenance would have had to be abandoned under Article 85 of the Treaty of Rome. It is likely that had the negotiations been successful, the abolition of RPM in Britain would have been one item in a vast programme of readjustment measures, and would not have attracted the attention it did in 1964 as a purely domestic issue.

Given the advent of Heath, to a Department with a fully-matured legislative policy, it remained for the Cabinet and the Prime Minister to be convinced, and from the autumn of 1963 the situation in this respect had become much more favourable. Macmillan, as well as having personal and political prejudices in favour of RPM, was also interested in economic policy, and would not give to a President of the Board of Trade as much freedom of manoeuvre as would a Prime Minister less well-versed in economic affairs. The new Prime Minister, Sir Alec Douglas Home, was a self-confessed novice in these matters, and with Maudling, an ex-Board of Trade President and instigator of the 1960 fact-finding enquiry into RPM as Chancellor of the Exchequer in the new Cabinet, Heath was assured of approval for his Bill. All the signs are that the Cabinet and Prime Minister were led by Heath and Maudling on this issue, and the Bill to abolish RPM was introduced in February, 1964.

There are grounds for thinking that the Government did not intend to act against price maintenance until after the 1964 General Election, and the decision to bring in hurried pre-election legislation on RPM was an electoral gamble. It was hoped by its sponsors that the housewife and pensioner votes which the policy might win for the

Conservatives would outweigh the loss of support amongst traders and shop-keepers. The fact that both the Labour and Liberal parties were in general opposed to resale price maintenance, and hence would not afford political shelter to the Bill's opponents, was another obvious factor in the Government's calculations. Also the adoption of policy was hastened by the activities of backbench MPs—two Private Members' Bills were introduced in the 1963-64 session which bore on RPM—Mr John Stonehouse's Bill to abolish it outright, and Mr John Osborn's Bill on trading stamps.

One way in which the development of the Resale Prices Bill was not typical of the legislative process was the lack of prior consultation with affected groups, which, as will be seen in the next chapter, is usually a widespread accompaniment to the preparatory stages of legislation in Britain. The Government did not even issue a preliminary White Paper as a basis for discussion. The various retailers' pressure groups in favour of the retention of RPM were gearing up, not to fight a Bill at the tail-end of a Parliament, but to contest a party plank at the coming General Election, and were hence caught unprepared. Nor was there political consultation by the Government with the Trade and Industry backbench subject group of the Parliamentary Conservative Party, where it was known that much Conservative opposition would centre. The chairman of the group, in a Commons' debate on the Bill, declared that it came as a complete surprise. It seems, however, to have been welcomed by the party's backbench Finance group, which was actuated by wider economic considerations than the Trade and Industry group.

Although in one way the history of the Bill shows the underlying continuity in Departmental administrative policy, politically the Bill constituted a reversal of attitude on the part of the Conservative Government towards a powerful block of its supporters which, if widely publicized, would have led the Government into considerable political argument and wrangling, from pressure groups and its own supporters, whilst the Bill was in preparation. The pressure might have been such as to force the withdrawal of the proposals. In the circumstances the Government produced a *fait accompli*, and paid for the lack of consultation later during the Parliamentary stages of the Bill.

III

Consultation and the Role of Pressure Groups in the Legislative Process

ONE of the reasons why less stress is now laid on the formal institutions and procedures of British government is the comparatively recent discovery of the importance in Britain of 'informal' politics, especially the politics of pressure groups. In their particular con-nexion with legislation, the role of pressure groups in the process whereby a government secures a measure of consent to its legislative policy cannot be overrated, and a discussion of the function of groups is prior, both in time and importance, to a discussion of the formal-legal institutions which operate in the legislative sphere.

As Allen Potter remarks in his study of organized groups in British politics,[1] constitutionally the process of securing consent to government policy is a matter of Parliamentary party politics. 'The government derives its political authority from the House of Commons, which derives its authority from the electorate'. But, Potter continues, 'the acquiescence and co-operation of the governed is not secured simply by occasionally convincing enough electors to return enough MPs to maintain the Government. In supplementing the constitutional conditions of legitimacy, the relations between the Government and organized groups play a most important part'. The liberal-democratic theory of political representation, whereby political parties and MPs are regarded as the sole vehicle of political ideas and programmes, has given way to a more realistic view of a system in which pressure groups are regarded as a sensitive section of the machinery for the selection of issues and for ensuring the responsiveness of government.[2] Without their activity, S.E. Finer asserts, party rule would be 'a rigid and ignorant tyranny', and public

[1] Allen Potter, *Organised Groups in British National Politics*, London, 1961.

[2] As a result of the studies which stress the legitimacy of pressure group activity there has been an attempt to get away from the invidious connotations of the term 'pressure group' itself. Potter uses the term 'organized groups' to some extent to imply that their activity is legitimate. In a rather more equivocal study of the role of groups, S. E. Finer prefers the more perjorative term 'lobby', and objects to the use of 'pressure group' on other grounds. Harry

c

administration 'a rigid and stupid bureaucracy'. R. T. McKenzie echoes Finer and concludes that pressure groups taken together, 'are a far more important channel of communication than parties for the transmission of political ideas from the mass of the citizenry to their rulers'.[3]

British law facilitates the formation of pressure groups. The majority are unincorporated voluntary associations, subject to few legal or administrative restraints unless they are regarded as trade unions or trade associations, in which case they come under the Trade Union Acts. This legal immunity has stimulated the growth of pressure groups to the point where there are now many thousands of them in Britain, differing greatly in their size, wealth, influence, degree of organization and their objectives. All of them develop some relationship, of different degrees of intensity, with central government, which has often been instrumental in stimulating their growth.

Consultation with pressure groups in the process of policy-making has a long history in Britain, dating back to the late seventeenth and early eighteenth centuries. Later in the eighteenth century the Industrial Revolution proliferated professional and technical bodies; national trades' and employers' associations became an important part of mature British industry towards the end of the nineteenth century, and were followed by 'peak' groups such as the TUC and the Federation of British Industries in this century. Consultation by government with groups in the nineteenth century was intermittent and desultory; the modern practice of almost continuous consultation was begun as a result of government control over industry and commerce during the First World War (although some powerful modern pressure groups owe their existence to earlier state policies). Most war-time controls of all sides and activities of industry were self-imposed under government guidance through the agency of trade associations and trade unions, a process which was developed further between 1939 and 1945.

Eckstein, however, in his study of the role of the British Medical Association in politics, points out that the attempts made by various authorities to define both the characteristics of groups and their attitude to group activity by the choice of a single descriptive word cannot succeed, and he uses the conventional term 'pressure group' as a comprehensive description of groups which pursue political ends even though they may have other non-political aims, and which use either 'sanctions, arguments or petitions', in their political activity. This is the sense in which the term is used in this and succeeding chapters. For extended argument on the semantic problem, see H. Eckstein, *Pressure Group Politics*, London, 1960, pp. 7–11; S. E. Finer, *Anonymous Empire*, 2nd ed. London, 1966, pp. 1–5; Allen Potter, *op. cit.*, pp. 15–17.

[3] R. T. McKenzie, 'Parties, Pressure Groups and the British Political Process', *Political Quarterly*, Vol. 29, 1958, pp. 9–10.

The technique of rule through mass political parties which has developed in Britain in this century has changed the relations of pressure groups and government. The party situation is now quite different from what it was at the beginning of this century, when a developing party system failed to reflect many important political issues. Some early pressure groups, such as the trade unions, were forced to make primary political demands which the party system at that time failed to embody and present adequately. Now the acute competition for electoral support by active national parties means that neither main party can afford to ignore any important section of the population in its political thinking. Although there is now more pressure group activity in Britain than at any time previously, the activities of groups are now contained within narrow limits prescribed by a political system which attempts to base its popular appeal as widely as possible. Most major groups have obtained not only recognition, but also by now their main objectives, usually as a result of political action over a considerable period of time. Groups now direct their efforts largely towards the day-to-day adjustment of their relations with government—'alterations of administrative procedure, readjustments of licence provisions and redrafting of regulations' are some of their main goals. The lack of marked differences in the programmes and aims of the major political parties, which has followed the acceptance by the Conservative Party of the managed economy and the Welfare State; the structure of decision-making in the modern British governmental system, which throws an enormous amount of authority into the hands of the executive; the technical and managerial nature of much of present-day government—all these factors direct the efforts of groups towards the Departments rather than to the political parties and Parliament, and at the same time tend to determine the type of problem on which they are most freely consulted by the government.

So great has been the interplay between governments and pressure groups in this post-1945 period that some authorities have taken the analysis of this phenomenon further, and have concluded that it has changed the basic character of the British political system, from a comparative 'open' political society to one in which the main ties of political influence and responsibility are often seen to be between the government and organized bodies protecting sectional interests. S. H. Beer, in his study *Modern British Politics*, stresses the emergence after 1945 of what he calls 'the new group politics' in Britain, and characterizes group organization and its relationship to government as a type of 'functional' representation overlaying the normal representative system. W. J. M. Mackenzie has concluded that the role of organized groups in British public life means that 'we are gradually shifting back into a situation in which man is socially important only as a holder of standard qualifications and as a member of authorized groups, in fact into a new medievalism'[4] Jean Blondel has characterized the new political system as a 'corporate state', a form of neo-capitalism 'in many ways reminiscent of the medieval system of guilds and very different from the traditional model of free enterprize organization',[5] whilst the term 'syndicalism' has also been used to describe the relation between modern government and its separate, organized 'publics'.

On the other hand, these observers profess themselves, with varying degrees of qualification, relatively content with the balance which has been struck between the influence of pressure groups and the authority of government in Britain, and there is little evidence to suggest, at the stage of primary policy-making, at least, that the function of government is merely to 'register' decisions which are made by pressure groups. The power of political parties and governments rests on a much wider basis that that of even the largest organized groups, and group support is not, in general, overwhelmingly important to them. As J. D. Stewart concludes, after a study of the role of groups in relation to the House of Commons, 'if the only object of the party were to gain power, then it would merely need to act as a broker between competing groups. If, however, the party seeks to gain power for a purpose then it has the resources as well as the authority to resist the groups'. In addition, as Stewart remarks, long-standing Departmental and civil service traditions and policies serve to restrain the challenge of groups to the political system, whilst the power and organization of the British political executive, which often results in very strong Cabinet or Cabinet committee control over Departmental activities, limits severely the independence of particular Departments in their relations with pressure groups.

Two main categories of pressure groups can be discerned—sectional 'spokesman' groups whose function is to defend the interests of a section of the community, as well as often to provide common services for it, and 'cause' or promotional groups, which exist almost exclusively to further a particular policy, and whose need for political support if their ends are to be gained is greater than that of sectional groups.[6] Most of the larger, wealthy and well-organized groups belong

[4] W. J. M. Mackenzie, 'Pressure Groups in British Government', *British Journal of Sociology*, June 1955, p. 146.

[5] J. Blondel, *Voters, Parties and Leaders*, London, 1966, p. 223.

[6] Again, the existence of the two types of activity in one organization, and of groups which are not primarily oriented towards political participation, although they may occasionally exert political pressure, causes semantic difficulties of classification. The finer distinctions, are not, however, important in this context.

to the first category, and most of the well-established relations of government with groups are usually with organizations of this type, although promotional groups are often consulted on matters of social policy, the sphere in which they are most active.

What is the basis of the power which pressure groups of both types can deploy in their dealings with government? S. H. Beer explains it as the need of government for advice on, acquiescence in and approval of their policies. Under the heading of advice is included the statistical information which most groups and associations collect and collate, and without which the detailed administration of regulatory policies by the government would be impossible. It also includes the technical knowledge and skills of professions and trades, which the government needs to mobilize if workable policies are to be developed, and which no government, however large its specialist civil service or network of advisory bodies, can hope to master in the same detail and to the same degree of sophistication as the actual practitioners. Beer gives examples—Food and Drug Acts dependent for their technical content on consultation with the relevant trade associations; Construction and Use Regulations for motor vehicles dependent upon the advice given by the Society of Motor Manufacturers and Traders. These examples can be multiplied almost indefinitely. Under the heading of 'acquiescence' Beer notes the fact that many regulatory activities of the modern state require the active co-operation of groups in carrying out a programme of policy. Under the heading 'approval' Beer draws attention to the 'extreme hesitation of Departments and Government ... to confront an open and public break with producer groups', which he attributes to 'the widespread acceptance of functional representation in British political culture', co-existing with the equal acceptance of the usual constitutional doctrines which assert the primary importance of the powers of Parliament and Ministers.

Sectional 'spokesman' and promotional groups enter the preparatory stage of legislation in different ways, and at a number of levels. The process may begin by the mooting of a legislative project by a Department as a result of its administrative experience. The Department may invite the views of interested groups or set up a committee of enquiry on which either the appropriate groups are represented or which canvasses their views. A Department may initiate a Bill without prior consultation at all, although this is rare. A group may have had some success in influencing the decision to legislate. It can attempt to influence the formation of Departmental policy through its connexions in the House of Commons, especially through its relations with backbench subject-groups of MPs, and if it can persuade powerful Parliamentary opinion of the soundness of its views it stands a good chance of persuading a Minister. Once a decision to legislate had been taken, a Department usually consults widely before its proposals are publicized, most often with leaders of the appropriate sectional groups, but also, if the nature of the legislation warrants it, with promotional groups who have expertize in the subject. A White Paper may be issued as a basis for public and Parliamentary discussion.

The most effective time for groups to operate is after a decision to legislate has been taken, but before a Bill has actually been drafted and published. Once the Government has publicly committed itself to the main lines of a Bill, disagreement and opposition by interested parties can only usually be manifested by public or Parliamentary campaigns, which groups are not well-fitted to undertake. Given the structure of public decision-making in Britain, in which Parliament plays a distinctly subordinate role, this line of action is usually far less likely to be successful than attempting to persuade the Minister.

The most successful consultation, from the point of view of pressure groups, is that which occurs at the fairly mundane level of administrative detail, or in the preparation of minor Departmental legislation, usually of an amending type. Here it is more apt to use the term negotiation rather than consultation, since the group will almost invariably succeed in obtaining legislation to its liking. Negotiation is not an apt description of what happens when group meets Department on the occasions when major legislation is contemplated, and group wishes can be, and often are, ignored if principle is at stake. Yet even in important areas of public policy there will usually be consultation, leading to some measure of agreement. The Agricultural Bill, which embodied Britain's post-war agricultural policy, was only introduced into the House of Commons 'after prolonged discussions of the principles governing agricultural policy between the Minister of Agriculture and outside bodies. ... It was from the thought of the groups concerned as much as from the Ministry that the Bill emerged'.[7] As the Minister of Agriculture said in the Commons à propos of the Bill, 'In translating these principles into detailed legislation, the Government have been wise enough to keep in close consultation with the main representative bodies of the industry. I refer to the National Farmers' Union, the Central Landowners' Association, the workers' unions, and the professional organizations. We sought, and we used their collective wisdom, and, if Press statements are any guide, they indicated that those bodies welcome the Measure as being a workmanlike, and indeed, a sensible scheme'[8].

[7] J. D. Stewart, *British Pressure Groups: their role in relation to the House of Commons*, Oxford, 1958, p. 18.
[8] *H. C. Debs*, 432, cols. 626–7. Quoted in Stewart, *op. cit.*, p. 18.

Consultation is even attempted by Departments when an issue is so controversial that it is likely to be opposed flatly by the relevant groups, as for example occurred with the first Steel Nationalization Bill; consultation under these circumstances is a gesture only. Where there is a distinct party attitude on the proposed legislation then the function of consultation with pressure groups will be different, and limited mainly to the discussion of administrative detail.

This explains to some extent the experience of the British Medical Association during the drafting of the 1946 National Health Service Bill, one of the major measures of the post-war Labour government. The BMA is usually regarded as the archetype of a successful pressure group, and over the years it has developed an almost symbiotic relationship with the Ministry of Health. As an organization it was virtually brought into being and into its present shape by the extension of state medicine in the nineteenth and twentieth centuries. Its membership increased until it became the most inclusive and largest medical association, and its organization and internal structure were both tightened and differentiated to enable it to become an effective negotiating instrument at all levels of public medical politics. As Eckstein remarks of this development, 'In its present form as a vast, highly bureaucratized and wealthy organization, [the British Medical Association] is the creature rather than the victim of public medical policies; and far from being involved in constant warfare with the Ministry it is engaged in constant co-operation with it—a highly useful adjunct to the Ministry's machinery of administration which, had it not already existed, the Ministry would have had to invent'[9].

The Association's political power is considerable; according to Eckstein it influenced greatly the shape of the National Health Service as it emerged from the creative period of 1946-49, despite a Minister, Aneurin Bevan, who was fairly hostile to the profession, and despite setbacks to its position during the drafting of the NHS Bill in 1946. Its main channel of influence, as is the case with all British sectional groups, is through the appropriate Department, in this case the Ministry of Health. It thereby recognizes the logic of the decision-making structure of British government, which concentrates authority in Ministerial Departments subject to checks, of varying degrees of severity, imposed on them by the Cabinet and Cabinet committees. Like most pressure groups, the BMA exerts some influence through publicity campaigns and through Parliament, but 'publicity is used chiefly as a tactical weapon for nudging the Ministry into certain positions or whipping up a show of unity in the professions'[10]. Its parlia-

[9] H. Eckstein, *Pressure Group Politics: the case of the British Medical Association*, London, 1960, p. 48.
[10] Eckstein, *op. cit.*, p. 74.

mentary activities are more important than its efforts to mobilize
public opinion, and on at least one major occasion it has been successful in playing off the Ministry against its Parliamentary supporters
and has gained an amendment to official policy, but this was ex-
ceptional. By and large it concentrates its main pressures on the
Ministry of Health.

Here the range of relationships between BMA officials and Ministry
of Health civil servants covers almost every aspect of the working of
the Medical Health Service. According to Eckstein, the Association
is consulted on everything to do with the Health Service which is
not a matter of routine administration. There is, however, one important exception to its record of successful negotiation—the process
of drafting the National Health Service Bill itself in 1945-46, although
Eckstein regards this failure as 'a very special case'. The BMA did not
wholly oppose the proposals for a National Health Service which
had appeared in a White Paper in 1944, but it opposed a number of
aspects of them. It was represented strongly on a National Health
Service Negotiating Committee which was set up by the professional
medical bodies, but the Minister of Health, Aneurin Bevan, 'was not
available for negotiations'.[11] Instead the Minister held conferences on
the Bill with the interested parties and groups, including the medical
profession, but did not regard these conferences as negotiations. The
BMA was presented with a prepared Bill which was a *fait accompli*—
a duplication of the situation which had occurred with Lloyd George's
Insurance Bill in 1911. Some minor tactical concessions were made
by the Minister before the Bill was introduced into Parliament, but
more for the Department's purposes than to satisfy the BMA. Concessions were also made by the Minister during the Parliamentary
stages of the Bill, some of which were subsequently included in regulations made under the Act, or in the 1949 National Health Service
(Amendment) Act; but by and large the BMA's representations were
ignored at this stage.

After the 1946 Act had been passed, a crisis of confidence arose
between the Minister of Health and the medical profession, directly
attributable to the failure of the Ministry to consult with the Association at the preparatory stages of the NHS Bill. This largely explains
why the Ministry adopted a much more accommodating and conciliatory attitude after 1946 than it had done before. In regulations made
under the authority of the 1946 Act, Bevan, for example, backed down
on his attitude towards a basically salaried Health Service to the point
where salary as an item of remuneration for doctors in the Service
virtually disappeared,[12] and in prolonged negotiations with the BMA

[11] Eckstein, *op. cit.*
[12] *Ibid.*

the Minister conceded many points, some technical, others basic to the conception of the Health Service, and gave the Association an amending Act—the National Health Service (Amendment) Act of 1949—which guaranteed the concession.

In explaining both the initial reluctance of the Ministry of Health to negotiate the terms of the 1946 Bill with the British Medical Association, and the subsequent retreat by the Ministry after the Act had gone through from many of the positions which it had taken up, Eckstein offers a variety of reasons, from which he adduces some general principles governing the relations of sectional groups with central government. He regards the ignoring of the BMA's representations during the drafting stage of the NHS Bill as a special case, explainable by the importance of the measure. The Bill was a matter of high policy, on which a clear political mandate had very recently been given. The Labour Government, newly elected in 1945, was faced with a severe problem in attempting to cope with the large amount of far-reaching and complex social legislation it was committed to, in addition to the normal burden of Parliamentary work. The Cabinet had an overriding interest in getting the new measures on the Statute Book, which was manifested in the drastic overhaul of the legislative machinery of the Cabinet which it put in hand as soon as it attained office.[13] The programme which the government had set itself 'did not leave the Ministry much scope for dallying and dawdling with any BMA negotiators'.[14] Eckstein shows that the Ministry of Health was under the firm direction of the Home Policy Committee of the Cabinet during the preparation of the Bill, and that its freedom of manoeuvre was to that extent curtailed; whereas, once the primary political objectives of the 1946 Act had been achieved the Ministry was left comparatively free to deal with the Association in ironing out disagreements. The conclusion broadly appears to be that, when a Bill has a party political origin, and when it features prominently in the mandate which the party has secured from the electorate, then the authority of the relevant organized groups is at a minimum; and that by and large the power of sectional groups is more obvious in matters of administrative detail and at the stage of subordinate legislation than in primary legislation of the type of the National Health Service Act.

By and large, 'attitude' or promotional groups are consulted much less frequently by governments contemplating legislation than are sectional groups. They lack most of the political and economic sanctions which sectional groups possess; they are usually smaller in size, weaker economically and have a more amorphous membership.

[13] See below, Chapter V.
[14] Eckstein, op. cit.

The extent to which their views are canvassed is normally wholly within the control of the Government. Only when an issue lies outside the normal area of concern of British politics, and when no clear political lead is given by the Government, do strong opportunities occur for their influence to be exerted. This was the case, for example, during the long campaign for the abolition of capital punishment in Britain, which reached a stage of success with the Homicide Act of 1957, and in which the old-established Howard League for Penal Reform and the newer National Campaign for the Abolition of Capital Punishment played a subordinate but important part.[15] In bringing pressure to bear on the government such groups are placed at considerable disadvantages when compared with sectional groups. They are often not recognized as representing any affected interest, and usually they are unable to operate through the usual channels of power, the Departments of State, and are put to the difficult task of attempting to convert public and Parliamentary opinion and working through Private Members' Bills. Although this type of group 'rarely cuts a significant figure on the stage of politics', its importance in occasionally supplementing the activities of political parties and in presenting issues which otherwise might be ignored cannot be discounted. Recent examples of this type of group activity have been the sponsoring of the Medical Termination of Pregnancy Bill by the Abortion Law Reform Association, and the Bill to abolish hare coursing sponsored through Mr Eric Heffer, MP, by the League Against Cruel Sports.

The extent of the Government's consultation with groups is a function, not of its political weakness, but of its political strength. Secure in its monopoly of political authority, the Government can afford to consult group and Parliamentary opinion widely, knowing that, ultimately, its view of the matter can be made to prevail. Consultation is ordinarily undertaken not because a government or Department is weak and unsure, but in order to gain for a policy the widest possible consent before initiating the formal legislative procedures. It is a means of gauging the extent of the political acceptability of a legislative proposal, since large sectional groups in particular are sources of political intelligence, and consultation tends to lessen the area of possible subsequent Parliamentary conflict on a Bill. Over and above these reasons, there is a broader factor which has been characterized as the 'persistent corporativism' of the British political culture, with the acceptance of the type of functional political representation which pressure groups provide, and which attributes to such groups a 'right' to influence policy. Fully-fledged theories

[15] See, J. B. Christoph, *Capital Punishment and British Politics*, London, 1962.

of group representation may no longer be current in Britain[16] but the attitudes associated with them still exist, and a general consensus on the legitimacy of organized interests having a voice in public policy explains the widespread practice of consultation with pressure groups more satisfactorily than reference to the practical technical and political benefits which governments gain from it.

[16] See A. H. Birch, *Representative and Responsible Government*, London, 1964, esp. Parts II and III.

IV

Consultation and the Role of Pressure Groups in Delegated Legislation

THE term 'delegated legislation', although customary, is misleading as a description of Departmental legislation. As Eckstein has remarked, 'In Britain, the process of delegating legislation hardly involves delegation in any real sense, but rather a shift of responsibility from Ministers as leaders of Parliament to Ministers as heads of administration', and he continues 'Hence the staggering number of statutory instruments in this age of the social service state and party government'. Political control by the executive of the legislative process, and particularly control of the extent to which legislative authority is retained in its hands, is complete, and explains the predominance of delegated legislation in present-day Britain more satisfactorily than the more formal, and usual, explanations in terms of the technicality of the subject matter of Statutory Instruments (although much of it is technical), or lack of Parliamentary time to consider legislative detail. Ministers like to retain for themselves a considerable area of manoeuvre, particularly in relation to their advisory agencies and the Department's clientele of pressure groups; extensive enabling clauses in parent Acts procure this.[1] There is also often a conflict of pace and timing between the stages of major legislative projects. Political and Parliamentary considerations may dictate a timetable for gaining agreement on major principles, but scope must be left for lengthy consultations and negotiations at the level of detailed administration.

Consultation plays a greater role in the preparation of statutory instruments than in the preparation of Bills. Once the main lines of legislative policy are laid down in an Act, the task of putting it into operation, and making the machinery work, becomes, in practice, the joint responsibility of a Department and its clientele of groups. The existence of a strong political commitment on the part of the government may prevent negotiation with interested parties on matters of principle, as may strong inter-Departmental pressures and

---

[1] See *Report of the Select Committee on Delegated Legislation*, 1953, Appendix B.

the control exercised by the Cabinet over major legislative projects; once the principles have been secured, a Department is
generally allowed a free hand in administration, and may be ready
to concede a great deal in the course of implementing a
statute. Cabinet control over Departmental Statutory Instruments
is nowhere near as continuous and as detailed as over primary legislative projects; certain categories of Statutory Instruments go automatically to the Legislation Committee of the Cabinet, but the Cabinet
is by and large only interested in SIs which might give rise to objections
on constitutional grounds. Otherwise subordinate legislation is overwhelmingly a Departmental as opposed to a Cabinet function; control
over subordinate legislation is dispersed amongst Departments, and is
practically complete at that level.

Most pressure groups are organized to bring influence to bear at
the level of the Departments, and particularly at the stage of administrative policy-making—a recognition of the structure of governmental
power in Britain. The concentration of governmental activity at the
Departmental level in Britain is explainable by a variety of circumstances—the technicality of much social service and regulatory
activity, the very large range of political consensus which has emerged
in post-war Britain, which, in Eckstein's words, 'keeps most political
bickering within the range of administrative detail and prevents
violent—or "important"—political controversies from arising', the very
large volume of legislative authority enjoyed by Departments as a
result of wide delegations—all these factors lead to the bulk of the
work of government being done at the executive level, and to groups
being in the main organized to exert pressure at these points.[2]

As J. D. Stewart remarks, 'the aims of the group today are rarely
major legislation, but rather minor amendments to a given framework and the safeguarding of the group's interest within the framework. The group is more concerned with the politics of detail than
the politics of issues'. S. E. Finer, in a passage on the relations of the
Federation (now the Confederation) of British Industries with the
Government, remarks 'one comment must be made immediately—
and that it is to stress how rarely the Federation is arguing policy
and how overwhelmingly it is concerned with detail, technique and
administration', and Finer quotes the Director-General of the FBI as
follows: 'Of course the great bulk of the work of government is

[2] Eckstein also draws attention to the 'old Tory theory of authority', a
characteristic British theory by which is meant 'the tendency both in British
government and British voluntary associations to delegate inordinately wide
powers to leaders and spokesmen, to ratify decisions taken by leaders almost
as a matter of form, which affords such leaders a wide range of manouevre
when they come face to face in negotiations'. See Eckstein, *op. cit.*, pp. 24–5.

administration, not policy, and most of what I have called the FBI's policy work lies in the field of administration. . . . . Measured numerically, the bulk of our contacts with the Government concern relatively minor, though important, issues.'[3]

The general position of pressure groups in relation to delegated legislation is fairly clear as a result of Departmental evidence given to the Select Committee on Delegated Legislation in 1952-53. The Committee circulated a questionnaire to try to establish the procedure adopted by Departments in framing Statutory Instruments. Some Departments only reported on the internal procedures of the Ministry; others reported fairly frankly on the type and content of Departmental consultation with interests, as the following summary of Appendix B to the Committee's Report illustrates: (the names of some Departments have changed since 1953).

The Admiralty

Limited consultation, since most orders affect only the Navy, but some consultation when civil interests are affected. 'The other authorities brought into consultation by the Secretariat Branch vary according to the type of Regulation . . . and to the extent to which the outside public is affected'.

The Air Ministry

A Department 'not much given to legislation'. However, byelaws made by the Ministry under the Military Lands Act are prepared by a procedure which gives opportunities to individuals and public bodies to object.

The Ministry of Civil Aviation

'A proposed new Regulation is first discussed with any interested bodies such as Pilots' Associations, aircraft operators, trade unions, aerodrome owners, etc.'

The Ministry of Education

'. . . no body of Regulations is ever put out without full consultation with outside bodies concerned. . . .'

The Ministry of Fuel and Power

This Department gave no evidence concerning consultation in the process of drawing up Regulations, but reported that one factor which determined the Minister in making the choice of 'laying' procedure for statutory instruments, was 'whether persons or bodies interested

---

[3] S. E. Finer, 'The Federation of British Industries', *Political Studies*, Vol. 4, 1956, p. 67.

would have other opportunities [than through their elected representatives] of making their views known, for example at public inquiries'. Opportunity for consultation with and hearing representations from interested groups hence determine the form of the Parliamentary procedure on SIs which the Department inserts into enabling Bills.

The Ministry of Labour

'in many instances, of course, subordinate legislation is only initiated after discussion with interested bodies—commonly in our case with both sides of industry'.

The Ministry of National Insurance

The Minister has a statutory duty to consult with advisory committees. The National Insurance Act of 1946 sets up the National Insurance Advisory Committee and in general requires the Minister to submit preliminary drafts of all regulations to the Committee. The National Insurance (Industrial Injuries) Act of 1946 sets up the Industrial Injuries Advisory Council and requires the Minister to refer proposals for regulations to the Council for consideration and advice, except in cases of urgency. The Council differs from the Committee in that the latter can receive objections to proposed regulations in writing, and also hear oral evidence in support of objections. The Committee's Report on draft regulations must be laid before Parliament together with the regulations themselves. The Advisory Council follows a different procedure; it does not advertise or receive formal objections, or hear oral evidence; it acts more as a committee of experts.

The Ministry of Transport

'In many cases the Minister is required by statute, before making regulations, to consult with representative organizations, and it is settled policy in almost all other cases, before making general regulations, to consult the representative bodies concerned. Consultation includes also any other Government Departments believed to be interested, trade unions and other outside interests. Such consultation may take place for exploratory purposes before the regulation drafting stage is reached, after which, if the Department's legal advisers have not already framed the necessary draft Statutory Instrument (with explanatory note in appropriate cases) for circulation during the stage of consultation, they are next asked to do so, and, if necessary, the draft is circulated to those consulted at the earlier stage'.

The Home Office

'It is the general practice of the Home Office, that wherever practicable, outside interests which may be affected by the regulations are consulted informally. For instance—the associations of local authorities are regularly consulted in matters in which they are interested; in the case of regulations relating to safety provisions in cinemas, representative local authorities and the trade interests concerned are consulted; in the case of regulations relating to safety appliances on fireguards, trade associations and professional organizations are consulted on the technical issues which arise.

The purpose of all these consultations is to secure that as far as possible regulations are agreed with the interests who will be most affected by them, though of course, in cases of disagreement it is the Secretary of State who decides what provisions they shall contain'.

The Board of Trade

'Regulations were made after lengthy consideration, often with detailed consultation with the interests affected'.

The Scottish Office

'In many cases the regulations are then either published in draft or are the subject of consultation with the appropriate advisory body or with interests affected. In some cases—for example, consultation about Police Regulations with the Scottish Police Council—this consultation is required by the statute. In others—for example, consultation with the Associations of Local Authorities about regulations prescribing the rates of expenses to be paid to councillors—it is undertaken to enable the Secretary of State to consider any representations that may be made'.

The Ministry of Health gave no evidence to the Select Committee on Delegated Legislation concerning the scope and type of consultation with interests. The British Medical Association had little influence in shaping the main lines of the National Health Service Act of 1946, and it threatened to boycott discussions with the Minister regarding regulations made under the Act—its assumption being, realistically, that without consultation the regulations would be unworkable. After concessions had been promised by the Ministry, the BMA agreed to consultation, setting up a committee to negotiate regulations with the Ministry.[4]

There are numerous types of scrutiny and criticism which can be applied to subordinate legislation. For the constitutional purist, legal and Parliamentary controls are the most important. They are,

---

[4] Eckstein, *op. cit.*, pp. 100–1.

however, the least effectual. Judicial examination of subordinate legislation is rare, and only runs to formal questions of *vires*; Parliamentary controls are restricted to superficial examination of the text of SIS by the Select Committee on Statutory Instruments of the House of Commons, and to the comparatively rare, and even more rarely successful prayer or motion to annul an Instrument.[5] These institutionalized controls are formal and minimal in their effect. There are however, many other ways in which Departments are influenced in the exercise of legislative powers. Public discussion, the general opinions of trade unions, employers' associations and individual experts all influence the process, in addition to the consultation which is sought by Departments. The Select Committee on Delegated Legislation of 1952-53 took very little direct evidence of the extent and influence of consultation in the process of subordinate legislation, and showed scant interest in the work of pressure groups either at the preparatory stage of Instruments or at the Parliamentary stage when annulment motions are put down or affirmative notions debated—an omission which contributed to the thin and formal report which the Committee published. The Committee was interested almost solely in formal constitutional processes; control by widespread consultation with affected or interested parties was largely ignored. The Committee for example, did not link the fact that very few SIS are found to be defective or unwieldy by the House of Commons with the evidence of thorough consultation which is a feature of the preparation of most important regulations.

The evidence given by Departments to the Select Committee on Delegated Legislation said very little about the forms which consultation can take. Departmental practice varies considerably; it may be unofficial *ad hoc* consultation between the officials of a Ministry and their opposite numbers in an association or group, most often in the form of the group being asked for its reaction to 'hypothetical' circumstances. (Although there is no question of the invasion of Parliament's prerogative as there would be with a Bill, actual circulation of the text of an instrument seems to be rare.) Closer and more permanent association of a Department with expert and interested opinion is provided by the great number of advisory committees, permanent and standing, temporary and *ad hoc*, which are created by Departments. Lists of bodies attached to central Departments in an advisory capacity given in a PEP special study of the role of advisory committees in British government credited, for example, the Ministry of Agriculture with fifty-four such committees; the Ministry of

---

[5] See Chapter VI for an appraisal of Parliamentary procedures on delegated legislation.

D

Health with twenty-three; the Home Office with thirty.[6] In a reply to a Parliamentary Question in 1963 it emerged that a total of fifty-six committees of enquiry into social and economic matters alone had been appointed between 1958 and 1962.[7]

Advisory committees of this type can be consulted by Departments at any stage in the process of government—in the formulation of policy, in its application, or in the review of policy. In practice, and the technical nature of the subject matter of most advisory committees bears this out, it is at the stage of application or administration that they are most widely used. They are seldom brought to bear on subjects which are 'political' in the party sense. They deal on the whole with subjects, or aspects of subjects, to which Parliament and the political parties give little attention, but on which an administrative policy must nevertheless be formulated. As the PEP study of advisory committees comments, 'Where policy has emerged out of party conflict, advisory committees are weak'.

Most committees have an official element of Departmental civil servants, seldom in a majority, but whose membership is essential if close connexion is to be established between a Department and a committee, and if the committee is to be helpful in the actual issues of administration. The extra-Departmental membership can be of many types; some committees are composed entirely of experts; many, however, have lay 'representatives' of interested parties as members, and an element of negotiation is present in their proceedings.[8] The

[6] PEP. *Advisory Committees in British Government*, London, 1960, Special Study V, 'Advisory Committees in 1958'.

[7] See H. C. Debs, 2 April 1963, cols. 237–42.

[8] See K. C. Wheare: *Government by Committee*, Oxford, 1955, Chapter IV. For the representation of pressure groups on Departmental advisory committees see PEP, *op. cit.* The representation of the main sectional groups on advisory committees in 1958 was as follows:

	Number of committees on which the group was represented
Business Groups	
Federation of British Industries	21
National Union of Manufacturers	11
Association of British Chambers of Commerce	13
British Employers' Confederation	13
National Farmers' Union	16
Labour and Professional Groups	
Trades Union Congress	30
National Union of Teachers	5
Local Authorities' Associations	
Association of Municipal Corporations	16
County Councils' Association	20
Association of Education Committees	5

(From Political and Economic Planning, *Advisory Committees in British Government*, London, 1960.)

general advisory functions of these non-statutory bodies, with their influence on administrative policy, affect both the scope and content of subordinate legislation. In addition, many enabling Acts require Departments to consult, either with individuals, or interest groups, or statutory advisory committees.

The processes of consultation on administrative matters generally, and on the content of Statutory Instruments in particular, are functional responses by Departments to meet the extension of government authority into complex regulatory and welfare fields. As such, they supplement the 'normal' patterns of constitutional relationships, and in so far as they have been private and 'unofficial' have been largely regarded as extra-constitutional. It is submitted that the practice is now so widespread and influential that consultation, at this level, at least, now bids fair to become a constitutional convention of the first importance, and imposes a different view of the entire process of subordinate law-making. Despite the formal concentration of authority in the hands of Ministers, actual decision-making is now dispersed between a Department and its consultants. Because of their formal authority Ministers can retain considerable discretion in accepting the results of consultation; on the other hand groups and Departmental consultants have their own sources of authority, which serves to limit considerably the discretion with which the Minister has been vested. Formal-legal analyses of delegated powers seldom take into account the extent of the constraint which consultation imposes on what are often, in form, at least, very wide grants of discretionary authority.

The prevailing practice of consultation in the process of making Statutory Instruments inevitably means that more attention is paid to the views of pressure groups and experts than of MPs, a situation which arouses mixed reactions amongst Parliamentarians and academic critics. Aneurin Bevan made the stock charge, in evidence to the Select Committee on Delegated Legislation: 'It has been said ... that one of the advantages of present-day legislation is that Ministers consult all sorts of expert opinion and interests especially affected before they present the Orders to Parliament. This is all to the good as far as it goes, but it means that the only body which is denied the power to influence an Order except in the ways I have already described, is the House of Commons itself. . . . It should also be kept in mind that it is Parliament's function to protect the general interest, whereas the Minister will have been in consultation with special interests and very often these are of considerable power and influence in the community'.[9]

This statement by Bevan is subject to the exceptions of cases—

[9] *H.C.* 310, 1952-3, p. 145.

usually concerning important SIs for which an affirmative resolution of the House of Commons is needed—where the Instruments are laid in draft before Parliament.[10] Also, most Ministers are careful to explain their policies and important aspects of administration to the Parliamentary party, and as a matter of policy Statutory Instruments of political interest, such as those imposing or altering charges for Health Service prescriptions, would be submitted by the Minister to the appropriate Parliamentary backbench subject groups to obtain their views. As J. E. Kersell remarks, 'Without much question, comment made within the confidential atmosphere of a Committee will be taken into account by a Minister, who voluntarily presents for discussion his proposal concerning a statutory instrument, or who is invited there to explain a matter which has caught the Committee's attention'.[11]

Nevertheless, and despite the fact that MPs usually regard as a sound and proper complaint the fact that consultation with outside interests has not taken place, there has been considerable disquiet amongst academic critics concerning the extent of consultation with groups and advisory committees in the processes of subordinate legislation, as against the extent to which Parliament is consulted, and some of the proposals which have been put up for relating the practice of consultation to the main political and constitutional processes of British government recognize, by implication, its extent, even if they overrate its importance. One critic has dubbed the process perjoratively as 'Government in the inner circle';[12] another asserts that Parliament is deliberately kept at arm's length by tacit agreement of the executive whenever administrative decisions which rest on technical advice are made.[13] Professor Griffith wishes the process to be expanded, and its results linked to the responsibilities of Parliament: 'wherever possible, the opinions of the advisory committees, the organized groups and the individual objectors should be published and laid before Parliament ... by these methods, the procedures can be made more effective and more confidence will be placed in the discretionary decisions of the Administration. Thus can be performed that function of examination, criticism and defence which Parliament is unable by its nature and

---

[10] About one in ten SI's are laid in draft form.

[11] John E. Kersell, *Parliamentary Supervision of Delegated Legislation*, London, 1960, p. 65.

[12] Professor Ely Devons, 'Government in the Inner Circle', *The Listener*, March 27, 1958.

[13] Austen Albu, MP, 'The Member of Parliament, the Executive and Scientific Policy', *Minerva*, Vol. I, No. I.

in the time at its disposal to exercise'.[14] Similar attempts to reconcile
the two levels of politics are inherent in Professor Crick's proposal for more MPs to be appointed to Departmental advisory committees,[15] and in the recommendation, frequently made, that the
House of Commons' Select Committee on Statutory Instruments
should be allowed to widen its scope to investigate the 'merits' of
Departmental regulations, and to relate them to their background of
administrative policy.[16]

These proposals probably all suffer from the same defect of over-
estimating the degree of interest of Parliamentarians in the details
of Departmental policy, and of underestimating the bulk of work
which would arise if Parliament ever seriously attempted to commit
itself to its consideration. Nor do they discriminate sufficiently between the different *types* of decision-making process necessary in a
modern governmental system. The PEP study of advisory committees
referred to earlier regards the system of which they are part, together with informal consultation, as a necessary counter-system to
popular democracy as a method of policy-making in some spheres—
'a search for rationality' rather than a party-political approach to
the public imagination. Although the process involves pressure
groups, the form and purpose of consultation at this level makes
reasoned and responsible argument the best weapon at a group's
disposal. 'Advisory committees proceed by discussion and compromise; they can only have strong influence when non-party issues
are at stake ... when there is no great popular pressure on their
subjects'. The Study concludes that consultative processes are likely
to grow in importance, but makes no specific recommendations for
reconciling the two levels of politics. The implication is that they
are too far removed in pace, methods and subject-matter for this to
be either possible or desirable.

Countervailing and corrective elements are in any case present
within the advisory and consultative system. Professor Blondel notes
the fact that the penetration of groups into administrative processes,
not only as consultants but often as administrators themselves, has
blurred the distinction between the two 'sides' of government. 'The
intermixing between outsiders and civil servants has now reached a
point where the distinction between "administrative decisions" and
"decisions taken by private individuals" is more and more difficult and
more useless to make'.[17] The implication of this analysis, and also of

---

[14] J. A. G. Griffith and H. Street, *Principles of Administrative Law*, 2nd ed.,
London, 1951, p. 141.
[15] Bernard Crick, *The Reform of Parliament*, Anchor ed. 1965, Chapter 8.
[16] See Chapter VII.
[17] J. Blondel, *Voters, Parties and Leaders*, London, 1963, p. 224.

Professor Rose's description of British government as 'composite government',[18] is the necessary assumption of some continuing responsibility for the acceptability of the results of consultation by interest groups.

Harry Eckstein, quite reasonably, sees no dangers in the customary secrecy which attends the negotiations of Departments and pressure groups. 'Who would take much interest in these transactions? Negotiations nowadays tend to be confidential not so much because of any anti-democratic collusion among the negotiators, but, much more important, because very few people really care about them. Nor is it really a bad thing. It is the result of the same factors which maximize pressure group activity and pressure group influence; a high degree of consensus on fundamental policy and the shift of disputes (partly because of fundamental agreement, partly for other reasons) to technical issues which most people do not and need not understand'.[19] Eckstein makes the point that there is a self-corrective factor in the process—he notes in his study of the BMA as a pressure group that whenever fundamental and interesting matters concerning the relations of the medical profession and the government have arisen, 'the normal machinery of publicity we associate with democracy has in fact swung into action, and negotiations have been well-aired (to their detriment).'[20]

Wherever, as in modern Britain, there exists a great deal of agreement on basic political issues, and a large degree of concern with narrowly delimited policies which impinge on technical fields, groups will emerge as important mediating agencies, 'defining opinion for government ... on a level upon which parties infrequently touch'. Although the bulk of pressure group activity does take place privately at Departmental level, '... it is not qualitatively important, however considerable in quantity; and it tells us nothing about the distribution of power between Parliament and Ministry for that should be measured only by taking account of really controversial questions of public policy'.[21]

---

[18] R. Rose, *Politics in England*, London, 1965, p. 213 *et. seq.*
[19] Eckstein, *op. cit.*, p. 158.
[20] *Ibid.*
[21] *Op. cit.* p. 20n.

V

Cabinet Control of the Legislative Process in the Primary Stages

IF consultation with pressure groups at the preparatory stage is one distinguishing mark of the British legislative process, Cabinet control of most of its stages is the other. The Cabinet itself does not now legislate—it is 'merely the decisive apex of a very complex structure of decision-making, involving all sorts of forces (the party in and outside Parliament, the civil service, pressure groups) that press upon the Cabinet and, by constant intervention, help shape the principles and details of legislation'.[1] Nevertheless, the Cabinet is the agency which controls this structure; its authority is often of a negative character, but is supreme.

Cabinet control over the legislative process is of three main types; it extends to matters of the substantive content of legislative projects exerted through its policy committees; to the actual form and wording of major Bills through its Legislation Committee, and invariably to the timing of legislative projects through a small Future Legislation Committee. This differentiation of the structure of the Cabinet for legislative purposes is comparatively recent, dating mainly from 1945, although it is part of the systematization of the Cabinet —the establishment of a Cabinet secretariat, and the division of work between Cabinet committees—which was undertaken after 1918 and which has served to strengthen and consolidate the power of the political executive in modern Britain.

The responsibility of the Cabinet for the general legislative programme to be put to Parliament dates back to before the 1867 Reform Act, and was a consequence of the concentration of the political life of the country into embryonic national parties, and the centralization of political authority in the Cabinet. On the other hand, formal Cabinet arrangements for the preparation of Bills and for the settling of the legislative programme date from later. They

---

[1] S. H. Beer and A. B. Ulam (ed.), *Patterns of Government*, 2nd ed., New York, 1962, pp. 135-6.

developed after 1867, and had settled into something like a routine by 1914.

In the late Victorian period, Cabinet committees were used for the work of preparing Bills which was too much for individual Ministers but for which civil servants (for constitutional reasons) could not be used. The outlines of the Bill disestablishing the Irish Church was settled in two sittings of the Cabinet and the detailed work on the Bill left to an *ad hoc* Cabinet Committee which included the Law Officers for Ireland and two draftsmen.[2] On the other hand, it was common practice for Ministers to tackle the drafting of clauses themselves, aided by draftsmen from the Office of Parliamentary Counsel to the Treasury, which was established in 1869. Gladstone himself drafted the first Home Rule Bill with the aid of the Irish Secretary.[3] By 1892, according to Mackintosh, Liberal Cabinets had developed a definite system. At the opening meetings in the autumn 'a list of measures was prepared and all the more intricate ones were handed over to Committees'.[4] This seems to have been as much a device to prevent Ministerial argument in full Cabinet as a functional way of relieving the burden of the Cabinet's work. Lord Morley in 1909 described the process: 'The Cabinet ... settles the principles of the Bill, then refers it to a committee of that body; the committee threshes out details in consultation with all the experts concerned and at command; the draft Bill comes to the Cabinet, and it is discussed both on the merits and in relation to parliamentary forces and parliamentary opinion.'[5] A little earlier Sir Courtney Ilbert, in his work on legislative drafting, said of the process: 'The amount of thought, time and labour which is bestowed on the preparation of the more important Government measures ... before they emerge to the public view is not fully realized. ... When it has been determined to give a measure a leading place in the Government programme of legislation for the session, and to press seriously forward, its preparation imposes a heavy tax on the time of the draftsmen and of the other officials concerned. The measure will often be referred to a Committee of the Cabinet, who will assist the Minister in charge in considering questions of principle. The first crude sketch will be gradually elaborated. There will be daily conferences with the Minister or with the permanent head of his department, or with both. There will be interviews and correspondence with experts in various branches of the subject with which the measure deals. Notes will have to be written tracing the history of previous legislation. . . . Each

---

[2] J. P. Mackintosh, *The British Cabinet*, London, 1962, p. 250.
[3] *Op. cit.*, p. 251.
[4] *Ibid.*
[5] Quoted in Mackintosh, *op. cit.*, pp. 251-2.

conference may involve a recasting and reprinting of the draft Bill, and successive editions will appear with bewildering rapidity'.[6]

It is apparent from these extracts that by the first decade of this century civil servants and Cabinet committees were used quite freely, although the machinery for operating below the level of the full Cabinet had not been completely developed. Before 1914 the Prime Minister and the Cabinet still took far greater interest in, and were far more influential in preparing, the main heads of most Bills of medium importance than is the case today, a situation which reflects the rather amateur and informal organization of pre-1914 Cabinets and the comparatively lighter load of administrative and legislative supervision which they were responsible for than that which is borne by modern Cabinets. The development after the First World War in the Cabinet organization for the detailed preparation and formal approval of Bills is in line with the general modern development of the Cabinet which is described by Mackintosh—an evolution from a governing institution to an appellate body, moderating and co-ordinating the claims of active Departments through powerful committees. Between the two World Wars, standing Cabinet committee arrangements were made to advise on Bills. This function fell to a Home Affairs Committee of the Cabinet, which had been set up in 1918 to prevent the small War Cabinet from being swamped by domestic business during the last year of the War. It considered all items of domestic legislation, both in their policy implications and their form and drafting. Some policy matters, when important or particularly controversial, still went to the full Cabinet. The Home Affairs Committee (its name was changed after the formation of the War Cabinet in 1940 to the Home Policy Committee) also planned and kept under review the Government's legislative programme for a Parliamentary session. In 1940 the functions of supervising form and policy were separated, a separate Legislation Committee of the Cabinet being devised for the task of scrutinizing the detailed form of Bills, and to plan a legislative programme.

After the war the Cabinet legislative organization was still further differentiated. In 1945 the Labour Government, with a large and pressing legislative programme to achieve, took the legislative arrangements of the Cabinet in hand, and remodelled the machinery of legislative planning. As Lord Morrison has recounted in his study *Government and Parliament*[7] in 1945 the functions of the Legislation

[6] Sir Courtney Ilbert, *Legislative Methods and Forms*, London, 1901, pp. 87–8.
[7] Lord Morrison of Lambeth, *Government and Parliament*, 3rd edition, London, 1964, Chapter XI, 'The Legislative Programme'. The following section leans heavily on Lord Morrison's account of the legislative organization of the Cabinet between 1945 and 1951.

Committee were split, and the important task of planning the content and strategy of the legislative programme for both individual Parliamentary sessions and the full five years of a Parliament was given to a new and small Future Legislation Committee, with Morrison, as Leader of the House of Commons, as chairman of both the new Committee and the Legislation Committee. This legislative structure seems to have lasted in essence, although later governments do not appear to have retained such a rigid distinction between the Legislation Committee and the Future Legislation Committee.

Present-day procedures in the Departments for preparing Bills are very closely geared to the procedures of Cabinet supervision outlined above. The normal practice now is for a Department which has obtained the approval of the Future Legislation Committee for a particular Bill to work out the heads of the Bill itself, as an instruction to Parliamentary Counsel. Most importantly, they will then be circulated to other Departments for observations, and to an appropriate policy committee of the Cabinet.[8] It is at this stage that the greatest degree of substantive Cabinet control is exerted, since it is through the agency of a Cabinet policy committee that inter-Departmental pressure to modify a Department's policy is applied. No Department is autonomous; Cabinet control is greatest over a non-Cabinet Ministry, whose political head lacks status, but in all cases Departmental policy has inter-Departmental repercussions which open the way to some limitation on a Department's autonomy. Eckstein, for example, in discussing the control exercised by the Cabinet over the National Health Service Bill of 1946, draws attention to the fact that 'The Ministry of Health is not the only department concerned with the administration of sanitary and medical policies. Its policies constantly touch upon those of other Ministries and must be co-ordinated with them: capital expenditures on hospitals impinge upon the jurisdiction of the Ministry of Works, sanitation policies upon that of the Ministry of Housing, employment policies upon that of the Ministry of Labour; and over all the Ministry's activities involving the expenditure of money and bearing upon economic policy in the larger sense looms the omnipresent Treasury, the chief co-ordinating Department, with its comprehensive powers over Departmental budgets and its formal power to give or deny prior approval to a Depart-

---

[8] The Committee structure of the Cabinet is seldom known in its entirety; in any case it is partly fluctuating. At times probably more than two dozen committees are at work, and some may be divided into sub-committees. Some, like the Defence and Home Policy Committees, are thoroughly institutionalized and are renewed by each Cabinet. Morrison lists twenty main committees operating in the 1945–50 Cabinet, with some special committees and sub-committees in addition. See Morrison, *op. cit.*, Chapter 2.

mental project having a financial aspect'.[9] Even though the Ministry of Health at that time was a powerful multi-purpose Department, of Cabinet status, it had to submit to considerable control over the content of the NHS Bill, which considerably reduced the influence of the BMA in the preparatory stages of the Bill. Inter-Departmental pressures constrain a Department more effectively than does the power of the pressure groups which are associated with it, although the BMA had more chance of making its voice heard when the Minister was in the Cabinet and the Department was of Cabinet status than later, when the Ministry of Health diminished considerably in its functions and importance.

R. A. Butler's experience as Minister of Education during the drafting of the 1944 Education Bill was roughly similar; if anything, Butler stresses Cabinet interest in the details of the proposed legislation rather more heavily than in Morrison's account of the way in which the Cabinet dealt with Bills during his tenure as Lord President. Butler mentions the necessity he was under of gaining Cabinet approval of the main lines of the Bill, and full Cabinet approval of the final draft.[10] But the Ministry of Education in 1944 was of lower status in the government than, for example, the Ministry of Health was in 1946; its policies impinged on the interests of the Ministry of Labour, with its concern for the supply of trained manpower, and on those of the Treasury, which in 1944 was responsible for University education through the UGC as well as for customary financial control.

At some stage in the preparatory process a draft of a Bill will be submitted to the Legislation Committee of the Cabinet. After the reorganization of the Cabinet's legislative structure in 1945, the Legislation Committee was set up as a technical committee, with a membership larger and more expert than that of the Future Legislation Committee, and which reflected its task of advising on the form, wording and acceptability of a particular measure. It was chaired by the Leader of the House of Commons, and included amongst its members the Lord Chancellor, the Law Officers of the Crown, the Chief Whip and a limited number of Departmental Ministers. The Ministers whose Bills came up for discussion were also present, and Parliamentary Counsel also attended. The Committee thus contained elements which could examine a Bill from two points of view, the legal, and the political and strategical. The Committee would examine a Bill, in Morrison's words, 'not normally from the point of view of policy, but from the standpoint of general structure,

[9] Eckstein, *op. cit.*, p. 54.
[10] See R. A. Butler, 'The Birth of a Bill', *Parliamentary Affairs*, Volume II, No. 3, Summer, 1949.

proper legal wording, fairness, good sense in carrying out the intentions of the Government, and general acceptability as a working measure'.[11] Before publication in final form, some Bills might go to the full Cabinet, or again to the appropriate policy committee for final scrutiny. During the heavy legislative sessions of the 1945-50 Parliament, the Legislation Committee was hard-worked. Morrison shows how many drafts of the important Bills introduced during this Parliament were necessary: Coal Industry Nationalization Bill, thirteen; Transport Bill, twenty-one; Electricity Bill, fifteen; Iron and Steel Bill, twelve; Town and Country Planning Bill, twenty-three.[12]

The most decisive control which the Cabinet can exert is not however, over policy or form, but over whether a Bill shall find a place in a sessional programme. This decision is taken by a Future Legislation Committee of the Cabinet well before the opening of a Parliamentary session, and its decisions are usually final. Morrison recounts the considerations which determined the Cabinet in 1945 to improve its legislative planning structure. It was necessary for the Cabinet to escape Departmental pressure in determining legislative priorities, and the Future Legislation Committee of the Cabinet was devised as 'a small and impartial planning tribunal', free from Departmental constraints, and consisting primarily of Morrison himself as Leader of the House of Commons, Lord Addison as Leader of the House of Lords, and the Chief Whip.

The Committee planned the work of each session on the basis, firstly, of the annual legislation which has to be passed each Session (e.g. the financial legislation, the Expiring Laws Continuance Bill, the Public Works Loan Bill); it then made time provision for the major Government Bills needed to implement Labour's electoral programme. It next considered the large number of Departmental projects which had no particular political importance, and lastly provided for minor Departmental Bills to fill any gaps in the speculative timetable, after leaving a reserve of time for legislative contingencies. Since the Government's electoral programme had been a heavy one, the Future Legislation Committee also made tentative spacings of the major political measures over the five years for which it expected the Government to retain office. Morrison indicates the considerations which dictated the spacing of Bills. Social Service measures—National Insurance, Industrial Injuries, National Health —were given priority and put together in the first Parliamentary Session. The Town and Country Planning Bill, which was very long and complex, was settled for 1946-47. Coal nationalization was politic-

[11] Morrison, *op. cit.*, p. 250.
[12] *Ibid.*

ally urgent, and the Bill was settled for 1945-46. Electricity and Gas Bills completed the nationalization of fuel in 1947 and 1948 respectively. The nationalization of transport was postponed until 1947 by reason of its complexity, and the Steel Nationalization Bill was left until 1949 as it was not a definite part of the electoral programme and opened up complex problems of organization and policy. A large and comprehensive Representation of the People Bill was also needed to implement war-time promises.

The precise timing of these measures depended on the state of readiness of Departments which were primarily responsible for the Bills. The cycle of approval followed the pattern described above, projects being sent in outline from Departments to the appropriate policy committee of the Cabinet after informal inter-Departmental consultation. Support for a measure by a policy committee of the Cabinet would help to strengthen a Department's case before the Future Legislation Committee for having the Bill included in a sessional programme. This Committee, having agreed a rough programme on the basis of the essential sessional legislation, would determine with the Chief Whip the time on Second Reading, Committee, Report and Third Reading stages which the essential legislation would be likely to occupy, based on estimates of its complexity and controversiality and the time which would be occupied by consideration of the Lords' amendments. Armed with this indication of 'the limits of the practicable', the Future Legislation Committee, in Morrison's words, 'met a roomful of clamant Ministers persuasively arguing the case for the inclusion of their Bill or Bills in the next sessional programme'.[18] After such meetings the Future Legislation Committee would draw up a list of Bills for the session under the categories noted above; Ministers would again be placated; appeal from disappointed Ministers to the full Cabinet was possible, but appears seldom to have occurred.

It is Morrison's view that the Labour Government of 1945-50 organized its legislative programme better than any previous administration, and this seems to have been the case. The Future Legislation Committee of the Cabinet, which was largely Morrison's creation, drew its authority from its impartiality and also from the fact that it was known to be working realistically with the Whips' Office. Not only was the Government Chief Whip a member of the Committee, but his Private Secretary was also drawn in for his knowledge of the Parliamentary legislative machinery. The Cabinet Secretariat was also available for help; it services all the committees of the Cabinet.

Some idea of the sort of Bills which often fail to get a place in the

[18] Morrison, *op. cit.*, p. 245.

legislative programme for a session can be gained from an examination of *The Times* annual review of pending legislation. For example, immediately before the Session 1961-62 opened, it was reliably predicted that the Government was bringing forward for inclusion in the Queen's Speech a number of Departmental measures which included a Shops and Offices Bill, an Airports' Authority Bill (already foreshadowed by a White Paper), a Young Offenders' Bill based on recommendations of the Ingleby Committee, and a Bill to give effect to the recommendations of the Royal Commission on Common Land.[14] None of these succeeded in getting a place in the sessional programme, and were again brought up the following year.[15] In 1963 the Airports' Authority Bill had yet to be introduced, the Government pleading lack of Parliamentary time, despite the fact that backbench Conservatives were pressing hard for legislation. Nor had the Common Land Bill been introduced, although the Commission had reported in 1958.[16]

Some of the factors which determined the Cabinet's thinking on the legislative programme for the last few years should also be noted. For the 1961-62 Session it was reported that the Cabinet was taking on fewer legislative commitments, since it expected vigorous opposition from a newly-united Opposition. In 1962-63 the Common Market question was regarded as likely to take up considerable Parliamentary time, whilst in the 1963-64 session the Government had to devise a legislative programme which would fit its plans for a General Election. The 1964 Labour Government's thinking on legislation was quite obviously conditioned by the risk of trying to introduce highly controversial legislation with a bare working majority in the House of Commons. Also, as a fresh government with some large Bills promised, the Parliamentary Counsels' Office was likely to be overwhelmed with work. Together with an Autumn Budget in 1964, this determined that major legislation was not in fact introduced into the Commons until early 1965, although it was possible to make a start on some less controversial measures in the Lords.

The Cabinet and Delegated Legislation

Policy committees and the Legislation Committee of the Cabinet also have functions in relation to delegated legislation, and exercise control over both the type and extent of the delegated powers to be included in a Bill, and over the Statutory Instruments made by Departments as

---

[14] See *The Times*, September 25, 1961, p. 8.
[15] See *The Times*, October 8, 1962.
[16] *The Times*, September 19, 1963, p. 5. 'Many Bills compete for priority in next Parliamentary Session.'

a result of delegated powers. Evidence given by a number of Departments to the Select Committee on Delegated Legislation in 1953 sets out the practice which is followed in drafting the enabling clauses of Bills. In the Ministry of Agriculture and Fisheries, for example, the Departmental Division primarily concerned with the Bill formulates the preliminary ideas about whether the Bill is to contain detailed provisions or whether it should comprise general principles, to be later elaborated by detailed schemes or regulations made by the Department. Proposals put by the Minister to the appropriate policy committee of the Cabinet which is considering the Bill as a whole 'will frequently include recommendations about the general structure of the proposed legislation, such as whether it should include any substantial amount of delegated legislation provisions, and may also suggest whether such delegated legislation, especially if it includes financial provisions such as a subsidy scheme, should be subject to the negative or affirmative resolution procedure'. The Ministry of National Insurance, as it was then called, reported that questions of doubt about the scope and form of delegated powers would be discussed by the Minister and Parliamentary Counsel, and that 'finally, the Bill will go before the Legislative (*sic*) Committee of the Cabinet where such questions may be, and from time to time have been, raised'. Similarly the Post Office reported that the details of enabling clauses were settled between the appropriate Division, the Legal Department and Parliamentary Counsel, and that if anything unusual were being proposed the Minister would decide whether it should be brought to the attention of the Legislation Committee of the Cabinet. This evidence bears out Morrison, who says that it was under his chairmanship in 1945 that the Legislation Committee began giving 'special consideration' to the enabling clauses of Bills containing powers to make regulations. But this does not seem to be evidence of the development of a consistent philosophy on delegated powers; unusual instances of delegation would be brought to the Cabinet Committee, but by and large it appears that the extent of delegated powers was a matter for Departmental decision, taken *ad hoc* in the light of the special circumstances of each Bill.

Under Morrison, the Legislation Committee of the Cabinet also began to give systematic consideration to important Statutory Instruments. 'When Instruments were of importance, or likely to be controversial, and certainly when any principles of liberty were involved, we required them to be submitted to the Legislation Committee for examination as if they were Bills ... there was at times considerable argument, for we were rightly on the watch lest the Departments went too far or in case the proper rights of the subject were impaired'.[17] This type of supervision of subordinate legislation by the Legislation Committee appears soon to have developed conventions; from the evidence and memoranda submitted to the Select Committee on Delegated Legislation in 1953 it appears that the Minister of the initiating Department has discretion to decide whether or not a particular Instrument should be submitted in draft to the Legislation Committee of the Cabinet, except that the following types of Instruments must be submitted:

(a) all Orders in Council made under emergency or transitional legislation;

(b) all Statutory Instruments likely to affect a large number of Departments whose interests cannot conveniently be ascertained by direct consultation;

(c) all Statutory Instruments likely to give rise to criticism by the Select Committee on Statutory Instruments of the House of Commons;

(d) all Statutory Instruments involving any departure from precedent, e.g. in the type of penalties imposed, in the procedure relating to such matters as appeals, or in encroachments on the liberty of the subject.

The Department concerned with a proposed Instrument which falls into these categories prepares and sends to the Legislation Committee a memorandum explaining why the SI is required, and must obtain the Committee's approval before the order is promulgated.

From this it appears that the interests of the Legislation Committee in subordinate legislation extends mainly to matters of form and constitutional propriety rather than to policy content, and that there is, except under the heading (b) above, not much Cabinet interest in Departmental administrative policy at this level. Departments are hence more free to determine the details of SIs than the main lines of substantive Bills, and can settle, for example, the degree and intensity of consultation with affected groups and interests at this level of legislative policy-making more freely than when the content of a main Bill is being decided upon, when Cabinet interest and inter-Departmental pressures are more pronounced.

Commenting on the arrangements for Cabinet scrutiny of subordinate legislation from the point of view of form and precedent, Sir C. K. Allen, perhaps the most fluent critic of the extent of delegated powers in Britain, has said 'Cabinet committees are confidential bodies, and it is impossible for anyone outside them to know details of their procedure—for example, how much time the Legis-

---

[17] Morrison, *op. cit.*, p. 250.

lation Committee can devote to the examination of Statutory Instruments. It is easily understandable that a matter like the establishment of the Industrial Disputes Tribunal, which was done by Instrument and not by statute, would very seriously engage the attention of the Cabinet'. Allen is, however, not taking due account of the evidence when he adds that 'it is also noteworthy that, despite this preliminary [Cabinet] screening, a number of Instruments have come under the criticism of the Scrutiny Committee' (the Select Committee on Statutory Instruments of the House of Commons). Observers (apart from Allen) are largely agreed that the work of the Scrutiny Committee since it was set up in 1944 has not disclosed much in the way of irresponsible or careless handling of delegated legislative powers by Departments. An analysis of the work of this Commons' Committee will be made later, but it is worth remarking here that by the end of the 1959-60 session the Committee had found grounds for criticizing only 131 Statutory Instruments out of a total of nearly 11,000 which it had examined since it was set up. Most of these references were on very minor technical points only, on which there was scope for considerable argument between the Departments and the Scrutiny Committee, and even in those few cases in which it was alleged that a Department had exceeded its delegated powers, the situation was usually not at all clear-cut. Allen himself arrives at the grudging conclusion that 'there is some reassurance in the fact that the Cabinet of the day, so far as its hard-pressed time permits, is alive to the importance of minor as well as major legislation'.[18]

A word should be said on the advisory and drafting functions of the Office of Parliamentary Counsel to the Treasury, which has responsibility for the technical form and wording of Bills and some advisory influence on the drafting by Departments of Statutory Instruments. The position of Parliamentary Counsel was for some time in the nineteenth century an informal one, the counsel being merely the barristers who were usually employed to draft Bills for the Home Office. In 1860 a permanent Office was founded, and taken into the Treasury in 1869. All government Bills with the exception of Bills relating to Scotland and certain formal Bills are drafted in the Parliamentary Counsels' Office. The advantage of a central drafting office, instead of dispersing the task amongst Departments, are many. Given Cabinet control of a legislative programme, drafting needs can be geared into the strict sessional timetable for legislation, and the fact that all Bills are centrally drafted enables the order of their preparation and their completion date to be controlled in a way that would not otherwise be possible. There are, in addition, other substantive benefits—as a member of the Office has said, 'Any one mem-

[18] Allen, *op. cit.*, p. 120.

ber of the Parliamentary Counsels' Office, in the course of a few sessions, is likely to range over most of the field of government activity; and he thus acquires not only a general view of the law governing administration and a facility for picking up details of the particular branch in which he is interested for the time being, but also a knowledge of the policy, attitude of mind and personalities of the different Departments, which greatly facilitates his work'.[19]

As indicated earlier in this chapter, an approved Departmental Bill is drafted initially on instructions from the Department primarily responsible for it, but the Counsel at this stage play their part in securing inter-Departmental co-ordination on legislative measures. The Office of Parliamentary Counsel has wider responsibilities than merely following Departmental instructions. 'It is concerned with fitting the provisions of a particular Minister's Bill into the structure and form of the statute book as a whole and it has a duty, the need for whose discharge was indeed one of the main reasons for its being set up, to study the fitting of a particular Minister's requirements with those of other Departments'.[20]

Approval of the draft has then to be obtained from the Legislation Committee of the Cabinet. This is no formality; the draft is circulated by the Committee to Ministers of all Departments and to the Lord Chancellor and the Law Officers. In the case of important legislation, many re-drafts may be ordered by the Legislation Committee and in all cases 'direction on, say, three or four points is common, and may well modify the general conception of a proposal as the draftsman has pictured it and tried to express it'.[21]

Although the Parliamentary Counsel attempt to some extent to fit the clauses of a Bill into a structure which will facilitate Parliamentary scrutiny of its provisions, this consideration is not so important as the need to make the Bill an adequate vehicle for detailed administration. A legislative project may be conceived first in terms of either national politics, or, more usually, Departmental administration. But whatever a Bill's provenance, it is Counsels' task to apply drafting techniques which will secure the Act as a basis for administration, and render it, so far as is possible, litigation-proof; Parliamentary requirements come a bad third to these two predominant considerations. There is need to consider Parliamentary aptitudes and capabilities more in the drafting of legislation; the attempt to produce for Parliamentary consideration legislative projects whose administration will be inordinately technical and complex, and which are drafted with these considerations in mind, leads to such cases as

[19] 'The Making and Form of Bills', by one of the Parliamentary Counsel to he Treasury, *Parliamentary Affairs*, Vol. II, No. 2, Spring, 1949.
[20] *Ibid.*   [21] *Ibid.*

the Land Commission Bill of 1966, which was virtually unintelligible to lay Parliamentarians.

Partly due to the fact that legal training in Britain concentrates on common rather than on statute law, the legal profession has done very little to advance the art of legislative draftsmanship. There are no up-to-date manuals on the legal aspects of the problem[22] and no twentieth-century body of drafting theory that in any way equals Bentham's work in the nineteenth century. The problem is admittedly a difficult one, compounded by the fact that Bills must be drafted in the light of the knowledge that the courts will normally adopt a very strict canon of statutory interpretation. However, this aspect of the legislative process would repay detailed study and research, in the light of a strict analysis of the stages of the process and their differing requirements.

[22] The last manual to be published was Lord Thring's *Practical Legislation*, in the late nineteenth century. Sir Courtney Ilbert, another Parliamentary Counsel, published *Legislative Methods and Forms*, with a section on drafting techniques, in 1901.

VI

Government Control of the Stages of Parliamentary Scrutiny and Criticism

IN 1908 Josef Redlich, speaking of the wholesale changes in the organization and procedure of Parliament which had occurred in the nineteenth century, wrote: 'Parliamentary procedure is the only Department of State where the old conventions and forms have been ruthlessly set aside from motives of political serviceableness, and where the political division of strength has received adequate legal expression'. The Standing Orders adopted by the House in the last half of the nineteenth century by and large recognized that government in Britain had become party government, and that the dominant party could expect to control not only the workings of the executive, but also the deliberations—and, largely, the conclusions—of Parliament. Parliamentary procedure, in this light, is best seen not as a set of impartial rules designed to facilitate the transaction of public and private business, but as a political instrument largely designed to help the governing party to govern.

This is not to say that the control of Parliament by the dominant party is ever complete—the limits of control in the sphere of legislation will become clearer as this section proceeds. On the other hand realization of the extensive and permanent nature of the political control of parliament exerted by the executive has had the effect of altering the received view of the nature of its functions. Formal constitutional theories of the role of Parliament in the spheres of legislation and finance have tended to recede, to be replaced by more empirical and realistic assessments of what Parliament actually does and what it can be expected to do. It is now widely recognized, for example, that Parliament exercises little influence over public finance, the legislative procedure for which is firmly in the hands of the Government,[1] and Parliamentary control in this sphere has been transmuted into the impartial scrutiny of public administration, largely directed to attempting to ensure economical government. However, Parliament's most important function is now seen to be

[1] See G. Reid, *The Politics of Financial Control*, London, 1966.

that of general criticism, advice and publicity, especially as it remains
the principal forum in which the political parties carry on a continuous election campaign. At a minimum, the House of Commons
provides a communications medium for drawing public attention
to issues and policies, projecting broad party images and ultimately
influencing voters. It is not solely a party public relations body, however; it also advertizes differences of opinion within the parties, ex-
presses individual and popular grievances, and deals with many non-
controversial matters. In all these respects the traditional procedures
of question and debate are still of considerable importance.

The result of this analysis for the legislative process in Parliament
is significant. No one seriously believes that Parliamentary influence
over the programme of Bills introduced each session by the Government will be considerable; it is only very rarely that a Bill will be
withdrawn as a result of parliamentary pressure. A few Conservative
Bills met unexpected opposition in the 1950s and were withdrawn
—the Judges' Remuneration Bill in 1953, the Teachers' Superannu-
ation Bill in 1954, the Industrial Organization and Development Bill
in the same year, and the Shops Bill, 1957. But if a government fails
to achieve its programme, the Bills which are not passed will have
failed usually because of defects, sometimes inescapable, in the planning of the session's timetable by the government. The following
table, reproduced from P. G. Richards,[2] shows that, by and large,
governments have been able to achieve a very high proportion of their
programme:

GOVERNMENT BILLS

Session	Total	Passed
1945-46	85	83
1946-47	55	55
1947-48	70	68
1948-	1	—
1948-49	102	101
1950	39	39
1950-51	60	58
1951-52	61	56
1952-53	42	41
1953-54	64	61
1954-55	32	25
1955-56	68	65
1956-57	53	51

[2] P. G. Richards, *Honourable Members: A Study of the British Back-Bencher,*
London, 1959, p. 110.

It follows that much of the work of the House of Commons on Bills is to be read in the context of the foregoing—that formal support or formal criticism of a Bill is largely a party occasion, directed not to the rejection of a Bill but to the education of a wider public in the political stances of the vocal parties, or groups within parties. Detailed criticism related strictly to the purposes of the Bill, of a type which is likely to have some mild success, is reserved for the committee rooms—in the meetings particularly of the private backbench subject groups of the major political parties and Ministers in charge of Bills, or moved openly in the workaday atmosphere of the standing committee stage of legislation.

It will have been seen from an earlier chapter that Bills prepared by the Government are as complete as the available time has allowed for; that from their normally distant genesis to their publication the process of development has been entirely under the control of a Minister and the Cabinet; and that a finished and printed Bill represents perhaps a process of thought and a distillation of ideas, practical considerations, pressure group representations and advisory committee hearings which might, in total, have spanned a decade. At very few stages, if at any, will Parliamentarians have had a hand in this preparatory process. In nineteenth-century Parliaments Parliamentary participation in—even often domination of—the processes of investigation and selection which are prior to legislation was marked. Many of the major reforming statutes of the Victorian era were the direct outcome of the Reports of Select Committees of the House of Commons. The Select Committee was the normal way of doing House of Commons' business in the nineteenth century; Professor Crick has shown the extent of the use of this device by nineteenth-century Parliaments, before reliance came to be placed on Royal Commissions and Departmental Committees.[3] Even in scientific and technological matters which were the subjects of proposed legislation the task of prior investigation was given to Select Committees, and much technical factory legislation was often preceded by this type of enquiry, with volumes of complex evidence being taken and digested, such as the famous Committee on Accidents in Coal-mines of 1835, whose report ran to 360 pages, with an elaborate index and many diagrams.

The use of Select Committees of the House of Commons to ascertain facts before the introduction of legislation declined steeply towards the end of the nineteenth century. It was the victim of the rise of party organization and political control of the Commons by the Government after the 1867 Reform Act, and the creation of the

[3] Bernard Crick, *The Reform of Parliament* (Anchor edition 1965) Appendix 'A'. 'The Decline of Select Committees of the House of Commons', pp. 225–7.

modern civil service, which removed from Parliament most of its responsibility for the preparation of legislation. Civil servants came increasingly to do for governments what Parliamentary clerks had formerly done for MPs, and the initiative for the introduction of all major legislation passed to the executive. In so far as there is a 'deliberative' stage in the legislative process, this is now found much earlier than the Parliamentary stages, in the interplay between political parties, pressure groups, Departments and the Cabinet, which together form a complex legislative decision-making structure, involving a variety of social and political forces. As has been remarked, 'It is this constellation of forces, rather than any single body, which deliberates on legislation.'[4] Parliament is only one element, and normally a minor element, in this pattern. The government is to a very great extent independent of Parliament, yet 'willing to listen to Parliament—to take its advice, redress its grievances, cater to its preferences.'[5]

Parliamentary participation at the deliberative stages of the legislative process survives only in the present attenuated arrangements for Private Members' Bills, which add very little to the volume of legislation. It is doubtful whether their primary function is legislative. In his apologia for Private Members' Bills Professor Bromhead admits that the government is as fully in control of this type of legislation as of government-sponsored Bills; 'If we look back over the list of private Members' Bills that have been passed, we must admit that all the Bills passed have been acceptable to the Government of the day, in principle and in detail, and could therefore appropriately have been brought in as Government Bills. . . . The same results might well have been achieved with a much smaller expenditure of parliamentary time'.[6] Bromhead appears to conclude that the main function of debate on Private Members' legislation, especially on the large percentage of Bills which are not acceptable to the Government, and hence fail, is an educative one, and that it acts as a safety valve for frustrated backbenchers. This may be the case, but debates on Private Members' motions would probably achieve the same result. There is, as Bromhead points out, a fundamental error in conceiving of Parliament as a 'legislature' in the sense that the French Assembly or the US Congress are 'legislatures', with all that this connotes for the fundamental rights of private legislators. Except for a brief historical period in the late eighteenth and early nineteenth

---

[4] S. H. Beer and A. B. Ulam ed., *Patterns of Government*, New York, 1962, p. 163.

[5] *Op. cit.*, p. 141.

[6] P. A. Bromhead, *Private Members' Bills in the British Parliament*, London, 1955, p. 171.

centuries, Parliament has never been the initiator of legislative policy
—it has usually been concerned with scrutiny, criticism and debate
than with proposing legislation. 'Parliament is the body which dis-
cusses what the Government has done, is doing and intends to do . . .
its power and effectiveness in this sphere are in reality greater than
they seem to be but it can only have this power and effectiveness as
a partner of a Government enjoying adequate authority to decide
and to act'.[7]

Parliamentary Stages in the Legislative Process

The present main stages of Public Bill procedure in the House of
Commons were distilled from a much more complex and cumber-
some procedure which was evolved in an earlier period of the
constitutional development of Parliament. Its main transformation in
the nineteenth century was the procedural accompaniment to the
rise of a fully-fledged Cabinet system and disciplined party
majorities. The effective stages are four in number—Second Reading,
Committee, Report and Third Reading, which together are intended
to constitute sufficient opportunities for the scrutiny and criticism
of both principle and detail of a Bill.

The Second Reading of most public Bills is almost entirely an
exercise between the opposing frontbench members. Backbench
contributions to Second Reading debates are always made, but the
substantive proceedings are limited to the moving of one Opposition
counter-motion to the original motion that the Bill be read a second
time. The motion selected is invariably that of the official Opposition;
other amendments are put down, for propaganda purposes, to exhibit
the political stance of individual backbenchers or groups of Members
on particular aspects of the Bill, or to give advance notice of points
which will be raised and concessions which will be demanded from
the Government at the committee stage. These amendments are not
moved on Second Reading.

The main Parliamentary stage of Bills is the committee stage of
the House of Commons, to which the legislative proceedings of the
House of Lords are primarily an adjunct. Since 1945 a sustained
attempt has been made to take the committee stage of most Bills in
standing committee rather than in Committee of the whole House—
an attempt which for various reasons has not always been successful.
In Sir Gilbert Campion's words, standing committees of the House
of Commons 'have never quite fulfilled the hopes entertained of
them or given that relief which was expected of them'.

Although the main purposes of the committee stage of Bills are
fairly well understood they lack a degree of precision. It has never

Op. cit., p. 168.

been in theory fully clear whether its function is the technical one of shaping the details of Bills in the light of the collective wisdom of the committee's members, or whether it is to extend political advocacy and opposition beyond the Second Reading stage into the details of legislation. In their late nineteenth-century origin, when two legislative committees were set up in the Commons as part of a package of procedural reforms designed to lessen the possibilities of Irish obstruction[8] it was presumed that the committees would deal largely with non-political Bills, and that they would follow the investigatory procedure and have the wide powers of Select Committees. It was not until 1947 that the relevant Standing Order of the House of Commons omitted reference to Select Committee procedure, and recognized that for some considerable time the standing committees had modelled their organization and proceedings on committees of the whole House. Originally, too, the standing committees were specialized, both in terms of their subject-matter and their personnel. Two large Committees dealing with legal and commercial matters respectively were set up in 1882. The Balfour reforms of the House of Commons' procedure of 1906-7, which established the standing committees in their modern form, retained this element of specialization by subject matter and also provided for two categories of committee members—a large nucleus to be chosen with reference both to party strengths in the House and to the fitness of particular Members for dealing with particular types of Bills, and a small added membership. The Committees after 1907 never did specialize by class of Bill, however, and the distinction between an 'expert' nucleus and an added membership became increasingly unreal, since political considerations required that the main criteria for membership should be the relative strength of the parties.

In 1933 the wording of the SO which provided for specialization by class of Bill was dropped; at the same time the sos were changed to provide that the nucleus of the committees' membership should be chosen only in strict proportion to the strength of the parties in the House, leaving the expert membership to be added—a change which recognized the primacy of political considerations in the make-up of the committees. After 1933 the two-part selection process in any case ceased to have much significance, the Committee of Selection having strict regard to the composition of the House not only when choosing the nuclei but in nominating the additional members. The distinction between nucleus and added members was abolished in 1960, in an attempt to overcome difficulties which had been experienced in manning the committees.

[8] See Josef Redlich, *The Procedure of the House of Commons: a Study of its History and Present Form*, London 1908, Vol. I, p. 174.

Over their lifetime the committees have grown smaller and more workmanlike, and their number has increased. The present maximum size of fifty members is only about half the maximum provided by the Balfour reforms, and a quorum can be as few as twelve. There is no limitation on how many can be set up, apart from the physical difficulties of manning and accommodation.

The post-1945 reforms of the Standing Committee System

The main changes in the use to which governments put standing committees came about with the re-shaping of their operations and the distinct up-grading in their importance which was carried out by the post-war Labour Government in 1945-46. Although since 1936 the Standing Orders of the House of Commons had provided for all Bills to be automatically sent to a standing committee unless the House otherwise ordered (which it was expected to do only in the case of financial legislation and some technical Bills), the practice between the wars had been to retain politically controversial Bills as well as short and urgent legislation on the floor of the House. A scheme for accelerating post-war reconstruction Bills through Parliament was considered by a committee of ministers of the Coalition Government towards the end of the 1939-45 War, and the 1945 Labour Government set up a Select Committee on Procedure of the House of Commons 'to consider the procedure in the public business of this House and to report what alterations, if any, are desirable for the more efficient despatch of such business'. This Committee considered the war-time proposals, and with considerable government prompting produced appropriate recommendations. The main change was one of practice rather than theory—the Government's main proposal, endorsed by the Procedure Committee, was for all Bills to be referred to standing committee other than taxation and financial measures, short of urgent Bills and Bills 'of first-class constitutional importance'. Standing committees were thus to become the major legislative instrument of the House of Commons. At the same time the Government took fuller control of their proceedings by the adoption of the Application of Time Orders—the guillotine—for use in committee proceedings, primarily to enable the government to overcome the political obstruction which was expected in the case of its major legislative proposals. Actual allocation of time for sections of Bills was made the responsibility of a sub-committee of the standing committee itself.

The purpose of the changes, to quote Herbert Morrison, the then Leader of the House of Commons, was to effect 'a change in attitude ... it was necessary for the Committees to accept the view that they must do something like a real day's work when required instead of just a few hours. It was necessary to develop the doctrine and practice that the House should split up into committees to carry through Bills, which would otherwise have occupied a full House with a smaller output. Unless Standing Committees took this view any attempt to develop them into useful parts of the legislative process ... would break down'.[9]

There is no doubt that in the circumstances of the 1945-50 Parliament the standing committees fulfilled Morrison's hopes. All the major Labour legislation went to standing committee, the Allocation of Time Orders were used, with some reluctance, and against considerable opposition, on three occasions, with the result that a very large and complex legislative programme was disposed of in a way which would have been impossible without the reforms. However, since the post-war reconstruction period government control of standing committees has not in the long run been as marked as was originally hoped. In the first place, government domination of standing committee proceedings is only complete when the government enjoys a large or largish majority, and there have been a number of occasions since 1950 when this pre-condition has been lacking. It is significant, for example, that in the session 1950-51, when the overall majority of the Labour Government was only six, it introduced no controversial legislation and retained most Bills on the floor of the House of Commons.

Other factors have played a part in reducing the usefulness of standing committees to the Government. Members of a Committee tend to be rather more specialized than the selection procedure would suggest and now often consist of MPs who have asked to be put on for a particular Bill. In the words of Sir Ivor Jennings, 'this means that most of the Government members have axes to grind, either on behalf of particular interests or on behalf of their constituents. There is nothing, of course, objectionable in this arrangement, but it does mean that the broader view adopted by the Government (on behalf of the general consumer, for instance) receives less attention than it did, and that there are fewer members ready to obey the Whip without question. . . . Hence Ministers prefer to take complex and contentious Bills on the floor of the House'.[10] This is a tailor-made explanation of why, for example, the Conservative Government in 1964 did not send the Resale Prices Bill to standing committee, since the main centres of opposition to it were in its own party, and interest group pressure for detailed amendment was very great. Even so, the Government was forced to adopt a large number of amend-

[9] Lord Morrison of Lambeth, *Government and Parliament* (3rd ed.) Oxford, 1964, p. 223.
[10] Sir Ivor Jennings, *Parliament*, 2nd edition, pp. 270-1.

ments, although it saved the main principles of the legislation. Committees develop a corporate attitude which can be at odds with the view of the government, and given a working majority the government is usually more in control of the whole House than it is of a standing committee.

A further factor in reducing the usefulness of standing committees has been the difficulty of manning them, although, as Professor Crick has pointed out, figures of attendance can be misleading.[11] Morning Committee sittings, debar the part-time politicians from regular attendance, and committee work tends to fall to a relatively small proportion of Members who are willing to work full-time—the 'House within a House' of conscientious MPs. Moreover, standing committee work seldom gets the same publicity as proceedings of the House as a whole, and is not so attractive to some MPs as a result.

The Minister in charge of a Bill, his Parliamentary and private secretaries and one or both of the Law Officers are put on a standing committee. Government Whips are not usually appointed to committees, a factor which reduces the degree of government control. Any whipping of members is usually done by the Minister's Parliamentary private secretary. Defeats of the government in standing committee are however very rare; in any case they do not carry the same sanctions as defeat in the House, since a government will not resign as a result of an adverse standing committee vote. The Minister can always get a decision reversed at the Report stage.

Although the Government has control of a Bill whether all its stages are taken on the floor of the House or whether it goes to standing committee, most Bills do not go through without amendment. But the number and quality of the amendments are most often an attribute of Ministerial control. Often a Bill will be incomplete at its stage of introduction to Parliament—although, as mentioned earlier, the main deliberative stage of legislation occurs before Parliament is brought formally into the process. But although inter-Departmental consultation will already have taken place at the stage of initial preparation of a Bill and in the appropriate policy committee of the Cabinet, and although consultation with pressure groups will also have been usually thorough, many representations on the details of the Bill may still remain to be made, as will a number of last-minute drafting amendments. Much of the Parliamentary Committee proceedings is a 'Ministerial' stage where refinements are added and administrative oversight corrected on the basis of the printed and published Bill.

Such amendments are by definition 'non-political' and acceptable to, even when they are not actually sought and moved by, the

[11] Bernard Crick, *op. cit.*, pp. 86–7.

Minister in charge. More politically-important attempts at amendment arise from party organization on a Bill, and from the more hostile reactions of pressure groups. A party organization is formed automatically for the purpose of Parliamentary proceedings on a Bill, with its focus the relevant backbench party subject group. On most Bills the Opposition forms an *ad hoc* organization to draft amendments and have them moved in committee and to consider Government and other amendments that are put down. Membership of the working party will overlap the relevant subject-group, and contain many members of it. The working party will normally nominate a leader as the Opposition counterpart of the Minister in charge of a Bill, who will co-ordinate Opposition efforts and direct the campaign against the Bill.[12] A recent instance is the Conservative working party on the Steel Bill of 1966 which waged a campaign which lasted a record period in standing committee. Headed by Anthony Barber, it also contained MPs who acted as 'section leaders' on particular clauses of the Bill. Often such groups work in close co-operation with outside bodies, and occasionally with party research organizations.

The committee stage is usually the occasion for the introduction of amendments on behalf of affected pressure groups. Given the part-time 'amateur' nature of Parliamentary membership in this country, it is usually held to be a virtue that politicians have outside experience and connexions, and pressure groups usually have no difficulty in making the contacts necessary to enable them to have a voice in committee. Many sectional and promotional groups can expect to find well-disposed sections of opinion in one or other House of Parliament without the need to develop formal or overt connexions —there are, for example, MPs who are local government representatives, Catholics, Methodists, ex-officers, who can be counted upon to be *prima facie* well-disposed to claims made by bodies with similar memberships and attitudes. On the other hand, a few pressure groups have created or helped to create formal machinery to enable them to achieve representation in Parliament. For example, British scientific organizations, including the fifty or so research associations and the professional scientific and technological institutes helped to create in the early 1930s the Parliamentary and Scientific Committee, a crossbench unofficial Committee which draws its very large membership from both Houses of Parliament as well as from these outside scientific organizations. With a complex structure, and its own offices and secretary, the Parliamentary and Scientific Committee is a powerful Parliamentary lobby for scientific interests, with

---

[12] See P. G. Richards, *op. cit.*, p. 114.

a constitution which, *inter alia*, directs it to scrutinize all Bills with a scientific content or bearing.[13] There are other crossbench groupings, for example the non-partisan Penal Reform Group and the Parliamentary Medical Group, which bring together the core of MPs and Peers who take a special interest in these policy areas, and who act normally in close association with the relevant pressure groups.[14] All-party committees such as these are the natural focus of groups whose aims are largely not party political and who deal with matters which do not normally arouse party interest.

Many pressure groups elect interested MPs as members of their executive, and MPs welcome these appointments, and the help and information which a pressure group can supply. The appointment of MPs to honorary posts is also used by groups to secure representation, and these appointments are often multiplied within an organization for this purpose. MPs accept them often because of electoral considerations; conversely, MPs, as well as their value as spokesmen in Parliament for the group, often have expertise or experience which can be put to use by the group in its everyday business. Other devices used to gain representation range from the establishment of a Parliamentary panel, to the actual promotion by a group of one of its own members for election to the Commons, and supporting his membership if he is successful. An early example of group-sponsored candidates were the Co-operative MPs, since joined with the Labour Party. Most sponsored candidates are now put up through the Labour Party, and the procedure is most used by the Party's affiliated unions. The Labour Party has laid down conditions regulating this practice, in particular the amount which the sponsoring body can contribute towards an MP's expenses. The Conservative Party, on the other hand, has no system of sponsored candidates and its financial rules on election expenses inhibit the development of the system in the party.

As J. D. Stewart remarks, 'Group representation through individual MPs gives to the group a means of tabling questions and amendments and of making its views known. It gives the group a foothold in the House'.[15] But this is a foothold only; a group needs to develop closer and deeper contact with representative opinion if its views are to be

---

[13] See S. A. Walkland, 'Science and Parliament: the origins and influence of the Parliamentary and Scientific Committee'. *Parliamentary Affairs*, Summer and Autumn, 1964.

[14] Examples of crossbench groupings can be multiplied, see Allen Potter, *Organized Groups in British National Politics*, Ch. 15, and J. D. Stewart, *British Pressure Groups: their role in relation to the House of Commons*, Ch. 8. For the activities of the Parliamentary Medical Group, see Eckstein, *Pressure Group Politics*, pp. 77–8.

[15] J. D. Stewart, *op. cit.*, p. 159.

given weight, and this is usually done by attempting to develop links with the relevant backbench party subject groups. Many groups have developed these contacts rather than contacts with all-party committees of MPs since the party subject committees are more powerful in influencing Ministerial policy. Even the scientific groups since 1960 have tended to bypass the well-established Parliamentary and Scientific Committee in favour of the party committees on science and technology. 'It is the party, not the all-party, committee that is important ... for that is a form of machinery which has not been created by the group but by the party, and therefore the party is attentive to it'.[16] Group contact with and influence within a Parliamentary party committee is an important factor in the group's standing with the appropriate Minister—if the party committee is favourable to a group's point of view its authority in consultation with the Minister is thereby enhanced. The best example is that of the National Farmers' Union which since the war has developed very close links with the Conservative Party Committee on agriculture, possibly the most influential committee of backbenchers within the Conservative Parliamentary Party.

In an earlier chapter it has been stressed that consultation at the level of the Departments during the preparatory stages of Bills is the main aim of pressure groups. But groups view the decision-making structure of government as a whole, and consultation with Departments at the preparatory stage of legislation is not used alone. Parliament is another forum for group activity, but the Parliamentary activities of groups are usually part of an overall strategy. Promotional groups tend to use Parliamentary channels rather more industriously than do sectional groups, but all groups use all available channels of influence. The approach to the Government by a group through the medium of the House of Commons is a well-understood adjunct, which normally does not alienate the Government, to the approach through Whitehall, and serves the group's purposes in different ways. As Stewart remarks, 'The most important features of Parliamentary amendments from the group's point of view is that the Government is required to give a definite decision, backed up with a statement of its reason for that decision ... indecision is often the greatest enemy the group has to fight in consultation.... The Government cannot give a reply at once and in the short time available between the publication of a Bill and its committee stage it is possible for points made to be overlooked—not from malice aforethought but from sheer pressure of work'.[17] Some groups use Parliamentary agents to draft amendments, but the ultimate wording of an accepted amendment is always under the control of the Minister. The tactics used by

[16] *Op. cit.*, p. 159.   [17] *Op. cit.*, p. 67.

groups in moving amendments differ. Sponsored MPs are used by trade unions in tabling amendments; approaches to the party subject group will often secure an amendment moved in committee, provided that it does not raise issues on which there is a political commitment. Some groups keep in touch with both parties; needless to say, amendments which are moved by the Opposition are often no more than token protests. To be effective, the Minister's own backbenchers must be persuaded.

The continuation on a different level of the processes of consultation which began earlier is the explanation of most group-sponsored amendments moved by well-disposed MPs at the committee stage of legislation. To go further than this, and to challenge the Government on points on which it has come to a decisive conclusion, is another and much more difficult proceeding for the group to undertake. It is difficult to generalize about the conditions under which such challenges are likely to be wholly or partly successful. Most situations are unique, and the outcome of a Parliamentary tussle between the Minister in charge of a Bill and the pressure groups which oppose it, or more normally, specific sections of it, will depend much on the nature of the legislation, its political significance, the strength of the opposing groups, and especially the political weight which they carry with the Minister's own backbench supporters, the attitude of the Opposition and, in some cases, the personalities involved. The timing of a measure will also have some bearing. Ministers can often succeed with measures which are unpopular with special interests at the beginning of a Parliament, rather than towards the end, when the political situation is tending towards fluidity and when to court political unpopularity might have severe electoral consequences.

Professor Finer, in his well-known study of pressure groups in Britain,[18] attempts a few generalizations about the conditions under which special interests are likely to succeed or fail, although he allows that the occasions which will admit them are comparatively rare. He postulates the situation where a pressure group which has succeeded in gaining the support of a section of the governing party's backbenchers can threaten the Minister with a combination of backbench rebellion and Opposition support, in which case the pressure group will usually succeed in its aim. The best instance of this type of situation in recent years occurred during the Parliamentary stages of the Resale Prices Bill in 1964. As has been seen in an earlier chapter, there was little or no advance publicity about this politically and economically far-reaching Conservative measure, and no consultation by the Board of Trade with the affected trade associations' peak group, the Resale Price Maintenance Co-ordinating Committee, set

[18] S. E. Finer, *Anonymous Empire*, 2nd ed., London, 1966, Chapter 6.

up in 1960 as the latest in a long line of powerful defence organizations for RPM. When Edward Heath, the President of the Board of Trade, informed the House of Commons in January, 1964, that the government intended introducing the Resale Prices Bill, the RPMCC immediately went into action. It appointed a PRO and circularized MPs with pro-RPM literature and information. It appointed a Parliamentary Agent to draft amendments to the Bill when it appeared. It urged its constituent associations to lobby their local Members of Parliament in opposition to the Bill. It found ready allies in the Conservative backbench Trade and Industry Committee, which contained MPs such as Sir Hugh Linstead, in close contact with particular Trade Associations. Even before the Bill was published there were well-attended meetings of this backbench committee—Finer reports an initial meeting with over one hundred disquieted Conservative backbenchers present, at which Heath defended his legislative proposals in both principle and detail. Attempts by hostile groups of Conservatives to persuade the Minister to alter his proposals failed, however; no major concession had been made to backbench opinion when the Bill was published in February, 1964.

The main struggle to amend the Bill then centred on the Parliamentary stages. Opposition to the Bill grew in the Conservative ranks, who were fearful of its electoral repercussions. Finer records a meeting of the Trade and Industry Committee on the Bill which attracted two hundred Conservative MPs. Seventeen Conservatives adopted a motion to kill the Bill on Second Reading, and a very large number of Conservative amendments, many of them drawn up in conjunction with the Resale Price Maintenance Co-ordinating Committee, were put down for the committee stage. In this situation the attitude of the Labour Opposition became crucial. In general Labour approved the principles of the Resale Prices Bill, but its attitude towards various Conservative amendments was not known, and there was a definite possibility that the Opposition and the Conservative rebels might combine to defeat the Government on sections of the Bill. Moreover, Parliament had just entered a distinct pre-election period, and as Finer remarks, 'it was no part of an opposition's rôle to support the government against its own rebels'. Hence the Opposition abstained on Second Reading, and let it be known that it might join forces with the rebels on specific clauses in committee. The extent of the rebellion in the Tory ranks was shown by the vote on Second Reading—twenty Conservatives defied the Government Whip and twenty more abstained.

Faced with more than one hundred and fifty Conservative amendments at the committee stage of the Bill (which was taken on the floor of the House of Commons as a means of en-

F

suring the maximum government control of the proceedings) the Government was forced to adopt conciliatory measures. A Conservative backbench steering committee on the Bill was set up by the Leader of the House, reflecting all shades of Conservative opinion on the Bill, which immediately began negotiations with the President of the Board of Trade. Under this sort of pressure Edward Heath was forced to give way at a number of points—in particular the important 'onus of proof' clause in the Bill, whereby all RPM agreements were to be deemed illegal until exempted by the Restrictive Practices Court, was changed to allow resale agreements to run on until specifically made illegal after a court hearing—a very important change of emphasis in the Bill.

The Minister was forced to make other concessions in committee, as a result of the combined strength of the Opposition and the Conservative rebels, backed in many cases by the Resale Price Maintenance Co-ordinating Committee, and on a number of occasions the Government narrowly avoided defeat. A large number of major concessions had to be made to the Bill's opponents.

There have been other examples of this type of situation, in which the Opposition and government backbench elements have combined against a Minister and forced amendments to a Bill. The situation recurred on the Race Relations Bill of 1965, when the Conservative Opposition, and hostile Labour backbench groups supported by the Society of Labour Lawyers and the Campaign Against Racial Discrimination, came together to force the Minister to adopt the principle of conciliation machinery instead of criminal sanctions to deal with proved instances of racial discrimination.[19]

Finer cites also the converse general case, in which pressure groups attempting to amend a Bill are generally unsuccessful since the Minister in charge is able to play off their supporters against a combination of his own backbench support and Opposition support. Although in these instances it may be politically embarrassing for a Minister to get his way with the help of the Opposition, on occasion this is deemed preferable to giving way to pressure. On the other hand, the cases in which the Minister can rely on Opposition support are by definition rare; the usual position in which a Minister is placed is an indeterminate one, with the Opposition playing its normal role, and the outcome of the struggle being determined entirely by the usual balance of party alignments. In these cases the Minister is usually in a position of strength, since although the affected groups might oppose his policy their interests are probably safer with the government than with the Opposition. The Minister is then in a position to accept or not accept the case of special interests,

[19] See Finer, *op. cit.*, pp. 76-7.

whether these are put to him through the Opposition or through his own backbenchers. As Finer remarks, 'such matters depend on party, parliamentary and public opinion at any particular time. For predictive purposes, the situation is quite indeterminate'.[20]

The reasons why Ministers are so accommodating, even to hostile interests, during the Parliamentary stages of a Bill are many. Perhaps the most important is the belief that special interests should be listened to, that their concern with public policy which affects them is legitimate, and that their point of view may have much to be said for it. These considerations usually carry more weight than political considerations—some groups are undoubtedly in a position to embarrass a government by withdrawal of aid and support, but have to be pushed to extremes to do so; manifestly many groups do not possess such sanctions. On the other hand, no Minister wishes to alienate opinion, Parliamentary or otherwise, if he can help it; if concessions can be given without too much compromise of principle, the odds are that they will be.

The Legislative Process and the House of Lords

When the Bryce Conference on the Reform of the Second Chamber reported in 1918, three of the four functions which it attributed to the reformed House of Lords had to do with legislation:

1 'The examination and revision of Bills brought from the House of Commons, a function which has become more needed since, on many occasions during the last thirty years, the House of Commons has been obliged to act under special rules limiting debate;

2 The initiation of Bills dealing with subjects of a comparatively non-controversial character, which may have an easier passage through the House of Commons, if they have been fully discussed and put into a well-considered shape before being submitted to it;

3 The interposition of so much delay (and no more) in the passing of a Bill into law as may enable the opinion of the nation to be adequately expressed upon it. This would be specially needed as regards Bills which affect the fundamentals of the Constitution or introduce new principles of legislation, or which raise issues whereon the opinion of the country may appear to be almost equally divided'.[21]

The third legislative function attributed to the Lords is now a political dead-letter,[22] and emphasis is now rightly placed on those

[20] Op. cit., p. 80.
[21] Cmnd. 9038, 1918.
[22] For the way in which the House of Lords has interpreted this function since the Parliament Act of 1911 see P. A. Bromhead, The House of Lords and Contemporary Politics, London, 1958, p. 134 et seq. and Chapter 12.

powers of amendment which the House of Lords possesses and which serve the purpose of requiring the Government to reconsider detail and not principle in legislation. The first two legislative functions of the Lords have grown in relative importance since the Bryce Conference reported, as a result of the large increase in government business and the increasingly stringent legislative time-table in the Commons. The real value of the House of Lords in the legislative process is as an important factor to be taken into account in drawing up a sessional programme of legislation by the Cabinet, and as an adjunct to and an extension of the committee stage of Bills in the House of Commons.

The legislative procedure of the House of Lords is similar to that of the Commons, except that given these different functions of the proceedings in the Lords, more emphasis is placed on the committee and Report stages of Bills. Normally the House of Lords sits as a whole at the committee stage, most of the routine work being done by a core of sixty to eighty members. A considerable amount of expertize is available in the Lords on some subjects. It contains ex-Ministers with wide administrative and political experience, and the Law Lords are available on legal matters and points of drafting.

It would seem to be conventional that Bills which are first introduced in the House of Lords should be largely non-controversial between the political parties, and should not deal with matters of major policy, although this convention has occasionally been ignored. The practice of bringing non-controversial Bills to the Lords first, whilst the House of Commons is engaged with major measures, also spreads the legislative work of a Session more evenly. During the Sessions 1947-55 rather more than a quarter of all Government Bills were introduced in the Lords,[23] and this appears to be the usual proportion.

Precisely the extent of the benefit which the House of Commons receives as a result of this proportion of Bills being dealt with first by the Lords is conjectural. It does not seem to be the case that the Commons is willing to rely implicitly on the Lords' handling of legislative detail. Some Lords' Bills are not debated at any stage in the Commons, but those which are usually take longer in the Commons than they have done in the Lords. Bromhead gives examples— in the Session 1948-49, on all but one of the thirteen Government Bills introduced first into the Lords, the committee stage was longer in the Commons than in the Lords, and altogether the time spent by the House of Commons in standing committee or committee of the Whole House was fifty per cent longer on these Bills than the time spent in the Lords; the same was roughly true of the other stages.[24]

[23] Bromhead, *op. cit.*, p. 189.   [24] *Op. cit.*, p. 194.

In this Session the Lords were more actively engaged in committee work on the heavy Labour legislative programme; in the Session 1951-52, the House of Commons spent eight times as long on the committee and Report stages of Lords' Bills than the Lords had done. To what extent the burden of the House of Commons is thus reduced must remain speculative, but, in Bromhead's words, it 'does not appear to have been particularly impressive'.

It is in fact the case that much committee work in the House of Commons is caused by the representations of groups which prefer to work through MPs rather than through Peers, and which thus recognize the political primacy of the Commons in the legislative process, and this in itself is bound to make the Commons' committee stage more important and lengthier than that of the Lords. On the other hand, the Lords' work on legislative detail is of high quality, and despite the fact that a Bill is usually re-examined at length by the House of Commons, some of the impress given to it by the Lords will remain.

The House of Lords' action on Bills, especially that majority of Public Bills which the government has introduced in the Commons, differs essentially from action in the other House, and is a function of the subordinate political role which the House of Lords occupies in the Parliamentary system. For example, since a division on the Second Reading of a Labour Government's Bill would inevitably lead to its defeat, the Conservative majority in the Lords follows a policy of not voting against the Second Reading of the Bills which originate with a Labour Government, whilst Second Readings of Conservative Bills are a foregone conclusion. As a result, the committee and Report stages in the Lords assume particular importance; the Lords concentrate on legislative detail, and even here it is 'generally felt that majority votes of the House are not the best way of arriving at final decisions'.[25] Amendments are proposed for the Government's consideration, in the full knowledge that the Government will in any case ultimately prevail.

By far the most important function of the Lords' stages, especially the committee stage, is to carry on the processes of consultation and compromise which have begun much earlier. As such it is complementary to, and must be viewed in the light of, proceedings which began in the Departments and the Cabinet, and were then continued in the standing committees of the Commons. As Bromhead remarks, 'at every stage of the discussion of a Bill, both inside Parliament, and outside, both before the Bill has been introduced into Parliament and afterwards, the Government is hearing arguments from all kinds of people, from interested bodies, from disinterested persons, and from

[25] *Op. cit.*, p. 143.

members of the Commons and of the Lords on both sides, who may in some cases be speaking on behalf of interests outside. Sometimes the Government accepts the arguments which it hears, very often it rejects them, and very often it proposes some sort of compromise. Thus the contribution of the Lords on the committee stage must be regarded and judged as a part of a far-reaching process of discussion in Parliament and outside; it is complementary to, not distinct from, the other private and parliamentary discussions'.[26]

Motives in moving amendments at the committee stage in the Lords do not differ essentially from the motives of MPs in the Commons. They are moved with even less hope of success, and primarily to clarify the Government's intentions on sections of the Bill. Most amendments are withdrawn after an explanation has been given by the Government. Many are considered by the Government and accepted either later in the committee stage or on Report, and in all cases, 'the essence of the transactions is the attempt to find a compromise, or at least a solution which can be made to appear defensible and moderate'.[27] The main value of the Lords' committee proceedings, however, is that they allow the Government the opportunity to deal finally with matters which have been held over from the Commons' stages or which have been decided in the Commons in ways of which the Government disapproves. The time between proceedings in the Commons and the Lords' stages allows private discussions to take place, with MPs, with representatives of interested groups, with Departmental advisers and Parliamentary Counsel; the Government then makes its final decision on the Lords' committee or Report stage through the Minister in the Lords or the Peer in charge of the Bill for the Government. Such amendments moved by the Government are often very numerous, but seldom politically momentous. Recent scholarship has shown that the number of substantive amendments passed by the Lords to House of Commons' Bills has been rapidly declining.[28] Most amendments 'are not the work of lynx-eyed elder statesmen ruthlessly scrutinizing the work of the parliamentary draftsmen. They are the work of the draftsmen and officials, dotting the i's and crossing the t's of their work with rare pedantry and refinement'.[29]

The same author concludes that it is the deliberative function of the House of Lords, especially in those areas which lie outside the normal range of political opinion, which is nowadays valuable, rather than its legislative function; it has become 'the Government Department, as it were, principally concerned with modifications of moral

[26] *Op. cit.*, p. 143.   [27] *Op. cit.*, p. 143.
[28] J. R. Vincent, 'The House of Lords', *Parliamentary Affairs*, Autumn, 1966.
[29] *Op. cit.*, p. 483.

tradition, and for effecting and interpreting the general will ... on questions such as the Abortion Bill'.[30]

The Parliamentary Stages of Subordinate Legislation

The structure of Parliamentary 'control' of delegated legislation has grown up piecemeal. Most enabling Acts conferring powers to make subordinate legislation make provision for some Parliamentary approval of the ensuing orders and regulations, and stipulate for this purpose one or more of a variety of Parliamentary procedures. Although some minor Departmental orders are not required to be laid before Parliament at all, those which are in the main are subject to one of three main types of Parliamentary procedure (although there are numerous refinements of each). Some regulations are only required to be laid before either House of Parliament for information, in which case there is little that can be done about them by interested Parliamentarians except perhaps the putting down of a Question. Most Statutory Instruments, however, are subject to laying procedures which open the administrative policy which they embody to various types of Parliamentary scrutiny and comment. In addition, since 1945 the House of Commons has had machinery for scrutinizing all Statutory Instruments which are directed by the parent Act to be laid before the House, to ascertain whether they reach certain levels of legal and formal propriety.

The Donoughmore-Scott Committee on Ministers' Powers in 1932 was the first official enquiry into delegated legislation to recommend that a small standing committee of the House of Commons should be set up to consider the constitutional aspects of regulations and orders made under delegated authority by government Departments. Nothing was done to implement the Donoughmore-Scott proposal until the Second World War, which saw a vast extension of Departmental legislation made under the Emergency Powers Acts. As Herbert Morrison, then Home Secretary, remarked, it was necessary 'to give up part of our democracy in times of war and crisis'. Nevertheless, by 1943 a group of MPs—the 'Active Backbenchers'—had organized themselves in order to reassert some control by the House of Commons over the vast quantity of wartime subordinate legislation. After a considerable Parliamentary campaign[31] the group was instrumental in forcing the Government to accede to the creation of a Select Committee of the House of Commons on Statutory Rules and Orders (since 1946 this Committee has been called the Select Committee on Statutory Instruments, and is often referred to as the Scrutiny

[30] Op. cit., p. 484.
[31] See J. E. Kersell, *Parliamentary Supervision of Delegated Legislation*, London, 1960, Chapter 4.

Committee) with the task of ensuring that Statutory Instruments laid before the House of Commons reach minimum standards of conformance with the parent legislation, of cogency and of promptness in laying and publication by the sponsoring Department.[32] The Committee did a great deal of good work in its first years in tightening up the standards of Departments in their handling of legislative powers, and was instrumental in sponsoring the Statutory Instruments Act of 1946, which laid down rules for the printing and publication of Departmental legislation, and standardized the period during which Instruments laid before Parliament are open to Parliamentary objection.

The Select Committee also found many occasions during the transitional period from war-time Ministerial powers between 1945 and 1951 to refer Statutory Instruments to the House of Commons under one or other of its terms of reference.[33] But it now seems that the early pressure of the Committee on Departments has taken effect, and Departments are now fairly punctilious in their handling of legislative powers. There have been only very few references under some of the Committee's terms of reference—for example, only one case of an Instrument imposing a charge has been detected, and some of the Committee's terms of reference are probably now superfluous. The most important references which the committee makes to the House of Commons are in cases where it alleges that a Department has made an 'unusual or unexpected use' of its powers in making an SI, allegations which usually hinge on a difference of interpretation of a statutory provision between the Select Committee and the Department concerned. Although the Select Committee, aided by the Counsel to the Speaker, does its work most thoroughly, it is now only occasionally that the House of Commons takes up these references to minor and usually unintentional breaches of statute by a Department. It is probably the case that the original Parliamentary sponsors of the Scrutiny Committee overestimated both the extent to which

[32] Summarized, the Committee's present terms of reference give it the authority to bring any Statutory Instrument laid before the House of Commons to the special attention of the House if it

    (i) imposes a charge on public revenues
    (ii) excludes challenge in the courts
    (iii) has retrospective effect
    (iv) has been delayed in publication or laying
    (v) has come into operation prior to laying without prompt notification to the Speaker of the House of Commons
    (vi) is not clear in form or meaning
    (vii) makes unusual or unexpected use of the powers conferred by the parent Act.

[33] See John Eaves, Jr., *Parliament and the Executive in Great Britain, 1939–51*, London, 1957.

powers to make subordinate legislation are abused by Departments, and also the extent of the interest of the House of Commons in these minor constitutional matters.[34] The Committee nevertheless follows conscientiously the rather negative and superficial role which its terms of reference condemn it to; it has very few constructive functions concerning the exercise of subordinate legislative powers by Departments, and its role is mainly deterrent, though probably still necessary.

Apart from its Special Orders Committee, which submits most SIs which are required to be laid before the House of Lords, and which have to be positively affirmed, to a similar sort of inquisition to that operated in the Commons by the Scrutiny Committee, the House of Lords has few functions in relation to subordinate legislation. Although the terms of the Parliament Acts do not extend to this type of legislation, the Lords rarely attempt to exercise any authority over the substance of SIs. The House of Commons, however, has well-understood procedures, which differ according to whether an SI has been laid under a parent Act which specifies an affirmative resolution for approving it, or whether legislation only requires that the House of Commons should have an opportunity of annulling it by a prayer to this effect moved by a Private Member. The latter procedure is the more common, and is used for SIs of medium importance. The much more time-consuming procedure of requiring a debate on an Instrument, followed by positive approval of it by a vote of the whole House, is retained for more important Instruments of the type which make financial provisions, or which bear very heavily on particular classes of the public, or which are very far-reaching in their general effect.

Government time must be allocated for affirmative resolutions of the House, and debate on them is to some extent constrained since there is no committee stage on SIs, and no provision for amendment. A government motion to approve must be opposed outright if criticism of an Instrument is to be made. With few exceptions affirmative resolutions are approved without division.[35]

Only superficial analyses have yet been made of the extent of opposition to SIs, particularly by prayers to annul, in proceedings in the Commons. However, the limits of Parliamentary 'control' in this sphere have become fairly explicit since 1945. The outright rejection of a Statutory Instrument is seldom obtained, and 'control' has come to be regarded as a process carried on almost exclusively between Government and Opposition, and limited to securing discussion of

[34] See S. A. Walkland, 'Unusual or unexpected use and the Select Committee on Statutory Instruments', *Parliamentary Affairs*, Winter, 1959–60.
[35] Kersell, *op. cit.*, pp. 88–9.

aspects of Departmental policy exhibited by the Instrument, the airing of individual grievances, and an occasional voluntary amendment of an Instrument by the Minister concerned. Kersell divides prayers against Instruments into two types: 'housewives' and 'lawyers', the former predominating in roughly a five to one proportion, and dealing with such matters as purchase tax increases, hire purchase regulations, schedules of transport charges, etc. 'Lawyers' prayers deal with legal and constitutional matters of the type which earlier may have involved the Scrutiny Committee; they are seldom pressed to a division, and are usually withdrawn after discussion and after the Minister has offered explanations and clarifications.[86] Debates on the merits of Instruments, however, are often pressed to a division, and require detailed explanations of Departmental administrative policy. They are often used to gain information in much the same way as are adjournment debates. Although they often divide the House, it is rare that a concession or amendment is obtained from the Minister, although occasionally opposition is bought off in this way.

It has been calculated that not more than one per cent of the total number of SIs that are made (which averages from 1500 to 2000 a year) in any way engage the attention of Parliament.[87] Sir C. K. Allen concludes 'It is then in the realm of constitutional fiction to say that Parliament exercises any really effective safeguards over delegated legislation'.[88] On the other hand, it is difficult to imagine any development of Parliamentary supervision which might not defeat many of the objects of delegation itself. There is, moreover, evidence that controversial subordinate legislation, of a type which might engage political feeling, is often brought to the Parliamentary party of the Government in its formative stages, and presumably influenced occasionally by backbench opinion. Much of the rest is not of the type which would interest MPs, who would have little to contribute even if their facilities for criticism were improved.

[86] Kersell, *op. cit.*, pp. 88–9.
[87] *Select Committee on Delegated Legislation*, 1953, Minutes of Evidence, Q. 792.
[88] Sir C. K. Allen, *Law and Orders*, 3rd edition, London 1965, p. 135.

VII

Proposals for the Reform of the Legislative Process

THE legislative process in Britain is the outcome of the total disposition of political forces in the country. Moreover, some of its characteristics, including the extent to which consultative procedures are resorted to in both primary and subordinate legislation, have their roots deep in the British political culture. It is not therefore feasible to conceive of the reform of the process as a whole, unless an entirely different political and constitutional system were to be postulated. Certain stages can be singled out, however, and various questions can be asked about the contribution of a stage to the total process. By common consent, the Parliamentary stages are those where reform would be most fruitful; the basic legislative procedures of Parliament, and both the type and extent of the attention which it pays to legislative projects, were largely determined in periods when the political and constitutional systems, and the place of Parliament within them, were very different from the present day, and little has been done to change the legislative role of Parliament since.

When Bill procedure in Parliament was stablized in something like its modern form in the latter half of the nineteenth century, various political factors determined its main characteristics and its comparative importance in Parliamentary proceedings generally. Government was then restricted to a few traditional areas. Legislation was the main mode of governmental action, whereas now it is often the last resort of governments whose major solutions to immeasurably more complex problems lie in the field of administrative and financial action. Richard Rose has remarked that nowadays 'legislative action is largely peripheral to much of the work of government'[1] and contrasts the present situation with that of a century ago, when 'an Act of Parliament extending the right to vote could be the

[1] Richard Rose, *Politics in England*, London, 1965, p. 208.
Rose makes his point by reference to the 1961–62 Parliamentary Session: 'In the parliamentary year October 31, 1961 to October 25, 1962, parliamentary legislation concerned such things as modifications in rates and methods of taxation, export guarantees, independence for various colonies, road safety,

primary policy problem of the year'. The content of many government policies was then relatively straightforward and well within the
competence of MPs. There was relative equality of opinion and
ability between Parliamentarians and civil servants; the executive
did not dispose of the vast formal and informal advisory structure
which it now possesses, and deliberation on legislation was not an
executive monopoly.

Yet there has been little fundamental change in Parliamentary
organization and procedures to allow the House of Commons to come
to terms with a modern process which is tightly controlled by the
executive, is often highly technical in its preliminary stages, and
whose end-product is often only the abbreviated expression of complex administrative reasoning. Parliament is still largely deficient in
facilities to enable it to scrutinize the technical and consultative
work of government; pressure for reform since the war has produced
some innovations, including a reformed Select Committee on Estimates, and the Select Committees on Statutory Instruments and
Nationalized Industries, all of which improve the investigatory
capacity of Parliament in specialized fields, but these developments
have been fairly opportunist, and cannot be said to be the result of a
systematic theory of Parliamentary organization for present-day tasks.

At present, Parliament spends more time on legislation than the
comparative importance of the process warrants. It also lacks
machinery to enable it to see legislative projects in the round, and to
assess the adequacy of the considerations and representations which
have been operative in the preparatory stages of projects. Most
schemes for reform of the legislative procedures of Parliament have
this latter consideration as their major premise. One category of
minor proposals, for example, has had as its object the provision of
more information for MPs concerning the purpose of and the reasoning behind government-sponsored legislative projects. Suggestions
for expanded White Papers to precede each Bill, explanatory memoranda for all Bills, expanded preambles to Bills and special memoranda to draw attention to the extent of delegated powers contained
in Bills,[2] all are evidence that the House of Commons has at times

---

the restriction of immigration from the Commonwealth. . . . But legislative
Acts could not cope with what the British government in the year 1961-62
regarded as amongst its major and immediate policy problems—the Berlin
crisis, negotiations to enter the European Common Market, the Cuban crisis,
disarmament and defence re-equipment, native unrest in Central Africa,
economic growth, wage restraint, inflation and urban congestion'.

[2] For details of these proposals see the Hansard Society publication, *Parliamentary Reform, 1933–60*, London, 1961, p. 64. This is a comprehensive if
undiscriminating summary of proposals for Parliamentary reform, but with a
minimum of comment.

felt a need for more explanations of the subject matter of legislation and the administrative activity which lies behind legislative proposals.

Much of the same sort of need is apparent in the many schemes which have been put forward for the reform of the standing committees of the House of Commons. There are proposals which take the present committee system as their basis, and modestly attempt to develop and extend it as the main legislative stage of the Commons. There have been proposals for specialized standing committees which would educate MPs in the complexities of particular areas of public legislation, and at the extreme there have been proposals which would merge the detailed legislative work of the House of Commons with committee machinery which would have as its primary task the supervision of policy and administration in a variety of fields of official action.

Schemes for the reformation of the legislative committee system of the House have been put to all the last four major enquiries into Parliamentary procedure—the Select Committees on Procedure of 1931, 1946, 1958 and 1964-65—by Clerks of the House of Commons and by academic critics. The proposals put by the Clerks of the House to the 1946 and 1958 enquiries were concerned with making the standing committee stage of the House of Commons the main legislative stage through which all Bills would pass; they envisaged innovations in the structure of the system and in the size of the committees, but did not propose radical alterations in their mode of activity or the extent to which the committees should be specialized. On the other hand, the proposals which were put to the 1931 Select Committee on Procedure on Public Business by the then Clerk envisaged radical changes in the standing committee system, entailing considerable specialization of both the personnel and the subject matter of the committees, and involving them in administrative and financial scrutiny as well as legislative work. These proposals were amongst the first to suggest the creation of specialized committees of scrutiny and advice in the Commons; they have since been built upon by numerous authorities, and have passed into the mainstream of modern thinking on Parliamentary reform.

Suggestions that the standing committees should remain unaltered except that they should each be allotted a part of the field of public business are open to the practical objection, as pointed out by K. C. Wheare, that the division of work between such committees would be extremely irregular.[3] Moreover, such proposals probably underestimate the extent to which the present committees attract specialist

[3] K. C. Wheare, *Government by Committee: An Essay on the British Constitution*, Oxford, 1955, p. 156.

MPs to them for particular Bills, and the potential for this sort of specialization has recently been increased by the abolition of the distinction between the nucleus of a standing committee and the added members. On the other hand, Wheare concedes that the present arrangement 'does not provide, through the standing committees, a steady education to members in a particular sphere of public business, such as would be provided if members belonged throughout a parliament to one or two specialized committees'.[4]

The suggestion, often made, that specialized committees of the House of Commons, with the powers and procedures of select committees, should be set up to exercise some degree of scrutiny and supervision over the administrative work of Departments has recently been accepted by the government, and a modest beginning with these new committees has been made. It has also been suggested that such specialist committees should be allowed to take the committee stage of relevant Bills, to avoid unnecessary duplication of committees dealing with similar subject matter. It is, however, highly unlikely that any Government, or, indeed, the House of Commons itself, would countenance the creation of such omnibus congressional-style bodies, although the proposals are logical, and to some extent overcome the objection that the work-load of specialized committees would be uneven.

Perhaps the most moderate and connected proposals for the reform of the Parliamentary stages of the legislative process to be recently advanced were those submitted in 1965 to the Select Committee on Procedure of the House of Commons by the Study of Parliament Group, a private association which brings together university teachers of politics and government and members of the Clerk's department of the House of Commons.[5] A number of the Group's submissions on parliamentary reform were accepted by the Select Committee, and ultimately, in diluted form, by the Government, and the Group has had some authority with Mr Richard Crossman as Leader of the House of Commons, himself a protagonist of moderate reform.

The Group's submission to the Select Committee on Procedure accepted as its datum the main lines of the British constitution as it has developed in this century, and stressed that 'the greatness and the unique character of British institutions lie in the fact that it has

---

[4] *Op. cit.*, p. 155.

[5] The submissions of the Study of Parliament Group were published as Appendix 2 to the *Fourth Report of the Select Committee on Procedure*, H.C. 303, 1964–65. They have also been published, with a commentary, by Political and Economic Planning, *Reforming the Commons*, by Members of the Study of Parliament Group, Vol. XXXI, No. 491, October 1965.

been possible and has for long been thought desirable to have both strong government and effective criticism of it within the House. But as the machinery of central government is strengthened, so steps should be taken to strengthen the critical efficacy of the House of Commons and its ability to reach the public ear.... So the kind of proposals we are making do not seek to change the accepted balance between the executive and Parliament, but rather to enable Parliament to perform its traditional role more efficiently and effectively'.[6]

The proposals which the Group submitted all assumed the continuing primacy and independence of government, with Parliament cast in an advisory and publicizing but not 'controlling' role. 'The procedures of the House of Commons need to be modified in recognition of the fact that effective "Parliamentary control" has for a long time meant not mainly the threat of overthrowing the Government in the House but also the process of influencing the Government and informing the electorate'.[7] The Group's memorandum concentrated on two aspects of House of Commons' business—procedure on public Bills and procedure relating to the investigation and scrutiny of policy and administration, although it also made a short submission on research and information services for MPs on the grounds that these subjects are not separable in any mature scheme of Parliamentary reform.

The central recommendation of the Group was concerned with rationalizing the division of responsibility in legislative projects between Parliament on the one hand and the Departments on the other, and most of the Group's other proposals were linked to this. The Group suggested 'that the amount of detail included in Bills should be reduced. Sections containing considerable detail, for example much of the matter at present included in the schedules to Bills, should be excluded from the text of legislation and left for treatment in statutory instruments. The extent of Ministers' powers to make statutory instruments should continue, as at present, to be defined in the parent legislation. Memoranda (for information only) should be attached to Bills indicating the scope and form of the delegated legislation that is envisaged'.[8] It is difficult to say whether the Study of Parliament Group is right in its contention that the House of Commons, given the present form of Bills, is called upon to judge matters in which it has no special competence, and which could be left for settlement by Departments. It would, however, be difficult to sustain the proposition that there is uniformity of practice amongst

---

[6] *Fourth Report from the Select Committee on Procedure, 1964–65*, Appendix 2, Preliminary Statement.
[7] *Ibid.*
[8] *Op. cit.*, para. 6.

Departments concerning the scope of enabling clauses in Bills, and delegated powers are often much less extensive in some Bills than in others. This seems to be entirely a result of Departmental tradition. As the Group said in a commentary on its submission to the Procedure Committee, 'at present it is often puzzling why some statutes contain remorseless detail and others simply give power to the Minister to make Statutory Instruments. These were once viewed as a threat to all our liberties. Without taking the matter lightly, one can at least recognize that delegated legislation has come to stay, that its application to one field more than another may seem no more than the preference of a particular Ministry or even of a particular draftsman, and that what is really required is more effective Parliamentary scrutiny of what happens once legislation becomes administration. . . .'[9]

Departmental evidence submitted to the Davies Committee on Delegated Legislation in 1953 emphasized the degree of autonomy enjoyed by Departments in determining the extent of delegated powers to be included in Bills. The primary decision lies with the Division of the Department which is responsible for the main heads of the Bill, with the advice of the Treasury Solicitor and Parliamentary Counsel, the latter occasionally having comments or advice to offer about proposals for enabling clauses in the light of his experience with comparable Bills. The Ministry of Health, for example, was quite explicit: ' . . . it is, of course, Ministers who decide what regulation-making power should be included in a Bill and what procedure should apply to any such power',[10] and it is obvious that Cabinet committee control over the details of the substantive clauses of a Bill is much more effective than over the decision as to what is to be put into a Bill and what is to be left to subordinate legislation.[11]

A number of Departments set out in some detail in their evidence to the Davies Committee the considerations which led them to decide whether to include matters in the substantive sections of Bills, or whether to leave them to be the subject of subordinate legislation, but in all cases the reasons hinged on considerations of administrative convenience or technicality and not on the wider grounds of Parliamentary aptitudes and abilities. The criteria differed widely from Department to Department, and no general principles can be adduced from the memoranda.

[9] PEP., *Reforming the Commons*, p. 282.
[10] *Report of the Select Committee on Delegated Legislation, 1953*, Appendix B, pp. 174–5.
[11] Only two Departments mentioned that enabling clauses which were in any way unusual would be referred for comment to the Legislation Committee of the Cabinet.

Professor J. A. G. Griffith, a joint-author of the submission of the Study of Parliament Group to the Select Committee on Procedure, has long been concerned with the anomalies which at present exist in the extent of delegated powers in Bills, and with the need to systematize and extend the practice of delegation on criteria which would primarily be based on the legislative capacity of the House of Commons. In an article on the subject published in 1951 Griffith showed through a number of case studies the wide differences which exist in a number of Acts of Parliament in the balance of substantive matter and material deemed fit to be dealt with by delegated legislation.[12] He concludes 'The principle reason for this failure to distinguish between those matters which are of general Parliamentary concern and those which should be left to Departmental regulation is not the haphazard nature of the growth of delegated legislation so much as the attitude of the Department to the nature of its drafting functions. To the Government a Bill is not primarily a document designed to enable Parliament to consider those matters which are its particular concern but a potential Act on which administration will be based'.[13] Griffith suggests a number of methods for overcoming this difficulty—that draftsmen should develop the principle that 'in deciding what should go into a Bill and what might be left for Ministerial regulation, the Bill must be regarded as a document to be submitted to Parliament for its consideration and not primarily as the basis for future administration', and that a Parliamentary Committee should examine Bills to see the extent to which this principle had been adopted and to bring pressure on the Government to alter its drafting conventions until they comply with this principle.

Similarly the Study of Parliament Group's recommendations would require the House of Commons to accept very wide delegations and to concentrate far more heavily on matters of legislative principle than is at present the case. The other side of the coin is some considerable improvement in the facilities of the House of Commons for arriving at the facts and opinions on which policy and administration are based, to enable it to sift the material on which substantive legislation has been built, and to enable it to scrutinize the administrative result of wide delegations of legislative authority. 'We consider that there is a strong case for streamlining the passage of legislation, but only if the consequence is to give the House more time, facilities and procedural devices with which to obtain the information that Members require and to study, scrutinize and criticize both the workings of the whole machinery of government

[12] J. A. G. Griffith, 'The Place of Parliament in the Legislative Process', *Modern Law Review*, Vol. 14, 1951.

[13] *Op. cit.*, p. 434.

and the factual assumptions on which policy decision are made'.[14] Here the Study of Parliament Group's recommendations join the main lines of recent reformist thought. The procedure of the House of Commons, since the development in this century of tightly disciplined Parliamentary parties, has become overwhelmingly adversary, a characteristic which has affected practically all the Commons' forms of proceedings; a common thread which unites all the major reform proposals of the last thirty years is the recommending of a more inquisitorial type of procedure, usually involving a change in the committee structure of the House. The SPG's recommendations are no exception, and its proposals to this end are worth examining at some length, since they have a particular bearing on the legislative process in Parliament.

The corollary of the Group's recommendation to restrict the House of Commons to matters of legislative principle, and to accept the principle of wide delegations to Departments (and in the Group's view, the probable precondition of the acceptance of their main recommendation) was the proposal for a new Select Committee of the House of Commons on the merits of Statutory Instruments as a means of achieving the purpose of the parent legislation, such a committee to be restricted to important Statutory Instruments needing an affirmative resolution from Parliament[15] and a few of those SIS submitted to the negative procedure in the Commons. The proposal envisaged that such a Committee would be a large one, with members added or discharged in respect of particular Instruments. 'The Committee should have power to appoint sub-committees, with the powers and procedures of Select Committees, to take evidence and report to the main Committee on particular instruments. The debates of the main Committee and the reports of its sub-committees (together with any minutes of evidence) should be published.'

This represents a fairly massive exercise on the subject of the merits of the more important subordinate legislation. It is not the first proposal to be made along these lines; a similar type of check was proposed by Sir Gilbert Campion, when Clerk of the House of Commons, in evidence to the 1946 Select Committee on Procedure,[16] where he envisaged that the task could be a possible extension of the work of the House of Commons' Select Committee on Statutory Instruments. This suggestion was taken up by critics who believed

---

[14] *Op. cit.*, Preliminary Statement.
[15] About one in ten of the Statutory Instruments laid before Parliament require an affirmative resolution.
[16] *3rd Report from the Select Committee on Procedure, 1946*; Additional Memorandum by Sir Gilbert Campion.

that without such an extension of its terms of reference the Select Committee on Statutory Instruments as originally conceived would remain narrow and legalistic in its approach to subordinate legislation.[17] Sir Gilbert Campion's proposal was briefly dismissed by the Government in 1946, on the ground that it meant that the Committee would be able to investigate Ministerial policy; the defenders of the scheme, however, have always insisted that an assessment of the merits of major Statutory Instruments as machinery for putting into practice a particular Departmental policy could be divorced from an evaluation of the wisdom of the policy itself. This could be a fine point, but even granting it, other objections can be raised. Presumably any examination of the merits of Instruments would entail an examination of the reports of Departmental advisory agencies and inter-Departmental committees, and also of any group representations which had been taken into account by the Department in drafting the subordinate legislation, and if a Commons' Committee was not satisfied that the ensuing Instrument tackled the legislative problem in the most apt way, it could only attempt to substitute its own judgement concerning the detailed use of the statutory powers for that of the Department. It is unlikely that any Minister would submit to such an invasion of his proper sphere of authority. Perhaps a better solution to the problem of how to assure the House of Commons that legislative authority retained by a Department in a Bill represented a proper functional assessment of matters which could with constitutional safety and propriety be left to executive determination would be better Parliamentary scrutiny of the extent and implications of enabling clauses when Bills are being approved, as suggested by Griffith, but the Study of Parliament Group made no recommendations to the Procedure Committee on this point.

The Group's recommendations for changing the committee procedure on Bills were moderate and in line with the general theme of its submissions. It advocated a pragmatically determined mixture of select and standing committees according to the type of Bill with which the Commons has to deal. Standing committees since their inception have developed a political procedure, although they began as select committees with investigatory powers. Although the present mode of proceedings of standing committees may be satisfactory for 'political' Bills, of a type which arouse strong party opposition, it is not satisfactory in the case of more technical legislation which may rest on complex and expert considerations which the House finds difficulty in discovering and assessing in the course of proceedings either on the floor of the House or in standing committee. For

[17] See A. H. Hanson, 'The Select Committee on Statutory Instruments: A Furher Note', *Public Administration*, Autumn, 1951.

Bills of this character, whose form has been largely determined by non-political considerations (and this probably applies to the majority of Departmental Bills) the Study of Parliament Group recommended a more investigatory procedure than that currently possible in standing committee. 'There should be some flexibility regarding the type and the size of committee to which any particular Bill should be sent. Most Bills would go to committees which would proceed in the same way as existing committees, but the membership might be as low as fifteen. Less controversial Bills, especially those involving detailed or technical matters, or Bills on which evidence from outside witnesses—either civil servants, independent experts or representatives of affected interests would appear valuable, should be committed initially to select committees more frequently than in recent years. Consideration of such Bills by select committees can lead to more relevant information being obtained and published (and hence to better informed debates), better drafting and closer agreement between the parties on what needs to be done. The work of the select committees on the Army and Air Force Acts, the Naval Discipline Act and the House of Commons Disqualification Bill, 1957, provide good examples of the value of this type of legislative scrutiny'.[18]

For the majority of Bills, however, the Group's proposals envisaged the continuance of the present non-investigatory system of standing committees, but its submissions on the committee stage of Bills were not divorced from its main submissions on the need to improve the facilities of the House of Commons for informing itself on the background factors which enter into policy-thinking of all types. This it saw as the function of new specialist committees of scrutiny and advice, of which it recommended five initially, to cover the policy areas of scientific development, Home Office affairs, the machinery of national, regional and local government and administration, housing, building and land use, and the social services. 'Specialist committees are needed to scrutinize the actions of government in their own fields, to collect, discuss and report evidence relevant to proceedings in Parliament, whether legislative or other. The main weakness in Parliament's present methods of scrutinizing administration, and indeed of debating policy matters, is the limited ability to obtain the background facts and understanding essential for any detailed criticism of administration or any informed discussion of policy. Specialist committees ... could go a long way to remedy this. They would be mainly concerned with administration and would normally seek to avoid matters of policy which are controversial between the major

---

[18] *Op. cit.*, 8(a). The Group's submissions contained also a number of points concerning the membership of committees. See para. 8(b) and (c) of the memorandum.

political parties. . . . Their reports would be fully argued and their evidence would be detailed . . .'[19] The Group envisaged that eventually the specialist committees might form at least the nucleus of the legislative standing committees, but the details of this were not fully worked out.[20] Formal arrangements for this might be unnecessary, since specialist committee members would inevitably seek to become members of standing committees for particular Bills which bore on the subject matter of their committee investigations. It was also proposed that the specialist committees would pay some regard to the operation of delegated legislation in their particular spheres of interest.

Some of the details of the Study of Parliament Group's submission to the Procedure Committee had not been fully digested, and might prove unwieldly in practice, but its perspective was both moderate and realistic and the philosophy of Parliamentary government which underlay the submission was impeccable. The proposals recognized both the complex and dispersed nature of the decision-making processes in modern British government, and within this system the connected nature of legislation and administration. They acknowledged that legislation is no longer the major mode of governmental activity, and that despite the large annual volume of legislation, it probably ranks less importantly in the range of processes for determining public policy than at any previous period. The organization and procedure of the House of Commons, however, still gives primacy to legislative proceedings; what is needed, as Griffith points out, is for Parliament to be regarded 'as a body which has certain functions to perform in the legislative process and that these functions should be determined by its nature and by the time which it has at its disposal. Other arguments based on *a priori* conceptions of sovereignty or on the idea that the executive is encroaching on the domain of Parliament by taking to itself legislative powers which properly belong to Parliament alone are both historically unsound and unsuited to modern conceptions of the nature of government. Moreover, these arguments, by insisting that Parliament should do more than it can and more than it is suited for, impede the necessary adaptation of Parliament to the new developments'.[21]

Over the last two years the Select Committee on Procedure has produced a continuous commentary on Parliamentary organization and procedure, and has examined the Study of Parliament Group's proposals on a number of occasions. By and large it has not been

[19] *Op. cit.*, para. 21(b).
[20] See *Fourth Report of the Select Committee on Procedure, 1964–65*, Evidence of Professors Bromhead, Hanson and Wiseman, paras. 229–30.
[21] *Op. cit.*, p. 435.

prepared to go as far as the Group in developing new assumptions concerning the legislative role of the House of Commons. However, the sum of the Committee's recommendations since 1965 constitutes a considerable revision of traditional procedure. Some of its proposals have already been instituted by the Government, in diluted form, and if recent recommendations of the Committee concerning Public Bill procedure are adopted, the comparatively simple legislative process in the House of Commons will become much more sophisticated, and the House will have greater investigatory and consultative opportunities in this sphere than it has so far possessed this century.

The Procedure Committee first touched on legislation in the 1964-65 Session. It made no recommendations at that stage for reform of the standing committee procedure of the House of Commons, beyond a time-saving proposal that in some cases the Second Reading of a Bill should be taken in committee, as has been possible for some time with some Scottish Bills in the Scottish Grand Committee. The proposal, which was accepted by the Government, envisaged that only Bills 'which are not measures involving large questions of policy nor likely to give rise to differences on party lines' should qualify for this treatment.[22] In its Fourth Report of the 1964-65 Session, the Procedure Committee took up the Study of Parliament Group's proposal for specialist committees of scrutiny and advice, with the powers of select committees, and recommended that they be developed initially as extensions of the Select Committee on Estimates. After a long delay, the Government accepted the general principles behind the proposals, and allowed the creation of two specialist committees, with possibly more to come in the future. Neither of these new Committees—on agriculture, and science and technology —operate in fields which are likely to give rise to much primary legislation, although both committees have had no hesitation in choosing subjects with a large policy content for their first investigations. Modest though these beginnings are, they signal an important constitutional innovation—the beginnings of specialization within the House of Commons—which ultimately might have implications for the legislative process.

More recently, the Procedure Committee has devoted the whole of a Report in the 1966-67 Session to Public Bill procedure,[23] and has recommended miscellaneous changes which in total are quite substantial, even if they do not add up to a completely consistent philosophy of Parliamentary participation in the processes of public

---

[22] *First Report from the Select Committee on Procedure*, H.C.149, 1965, para. 3.
[23] *Sixth Report from the Select Committee on Procedure*, H.C.539, 1967. 'Public Bill Procedure, etc.'

legislation. The Committee recommended increased use of Second Reading committees, which so far have been employed sparingly,[24] and with the same time-saving end in view, recommended taking some report stages of Public Bills and some prayers against Statutory Instruments in committee.[25] In line with the Study of Parliament Group's submissions, it also recommended increased use of Select Committees as an extra investigatory stage in the consideration of some Bills.[26] The more radical proposals of the Study of Parliament Group concerning the form of Bills and the need to confine Parliamentary attention to matters of legislative principle were turned down by the Procedure Committee, counter-arguments being brought by the Clerk of Public Bills and the First Parliamentary Counsel.

The Committee further proposed bringing the House of Commons into the deliberative stage of some types of legislation. It recommended that in general the House should spend more time debating legislative projects in their formative stages, either by debate on specific government proposals, or through *ad hoc* committees on future legislation.[27] The Procedure Committee also repeated its hope that the new specialist Select Committees would occasionally develop ideas for legislative action. The Committee saw this pre-natal function of the House as one which is more appropriate for non-party subjects of a type now dealt with primarily by Private Members' Bills, and these recommendations are probably the beginnings of a recognition that this type of legislation is getting beyond the capacity and resources of individual backbenchers.

However, when and if the complex question of Parliamentary reform reaches an outcome, the position will never be regained— nor should it—when Parliament can be termed in any but the broadest sense a legislature. The legislative process in Britain is first and foremost an executive process, and this it will, and should, remain. Parliament has many virtues and many capacities, particularly those associated with a wide and varied membership, an ability to reflect electoral fears and wishes, and to represent to a government the 'state of the nation'. Its capacity for detailed work of a specialist kind, is, however, necessarily limited by the capacity and experience of its members; it is far greater than most Ministers and civil servants would credit it with, and rather less than some Parliamentary reformers wish to believe. But policy needs to be developed and legitimized by the activity of an informed and representative assembly. To advocate changes that would ensure this is not to advocate

[24] *Op. cit.*, paras. 20–21.
[25] *Op. cit.*, paras. 25–26 and para. 32.
[26] *Op. cit.*, para. 23.
[27] *Op. cit.*, paras. 11–15.

Parliamentary dominance of what is and should be an executive function. It is, however, to attempt to add a realistic and powerful political dimension to the work of government. That is what Parliament exists for; that is what it often finds difficult to do at present.

RECOMMENDED FOR FURTHER READING

BEER, S. H., *Modern British Politics*, London, 1965

BLONDEL, J., *Voters, Parties and Leaders*, London, 1966; Baltimore, 1964

BROMHEAD, P. A., *The House of Lords and Contemporary Politics*, London and New York, 1958

BUTLER, R. A., 'The Birth of a Bill' *Parliamentary Affairs*, Vol. II, No. 3, 1949

BUTT, R., *The Power of Parliament*, London, 1967

CRICK, B., *The Reform of Parliament*, 2d ed., London, 1968; New York, 1965

EAVES, J., (Jr.), *Parliament and the Executive in Great Britain*, 1939-51, London, 1957

ECKSTEIN, H., *Pressure Group Politics*, London, 1960

FINER, S. E., *Anonymous Empire*, 2d ed., London and New York, 1966

GRIFFITH, J. A. G., 'The Place of Parliament in the Legislative Process,' *Modern Law Review*, Vol. XIV, 1951

HUGHES, C., *The British Statute Book*, London and New York, 1957

ILBERT, Sir Courtney, *Legislative Methods and Forms*, Oxford, 1901

JENNINGS, Sir W. I., *Parliament*, 2d ed., Cambridge, 1957

KERSELL, J. E., *Parliamentary Supervision of Delegated Legislation*, London, 1960

MACKINTOSH, J. P., *The British Cabinet*, London and Toronto, 1962

MORRISON OF LAMBETH, LORD, *Government and Parliament*, 3d ed., London and New York, 1964

POLITICAL AND ECONOMIC PLANNING, *Advisory Committees in British Government*, London, 1960

RICHARDS, P. G., *Honourable Members: A Study of the British Backbencher*, London and New York, 1959

ROSE, R., *Politics in England*, London, 1965; Boston, 1964

STEWART, J. D., *British Pressure Groups: Their role in relation to the House of Commons*, Oxford and New York, 1958

VINCENT, R. J., "The House of Lords" *Parliamentary Affairs*, Vol. XIX, No. 4, 1966

Report of the Select Committee on Delegated Legislation, H. C. 310-1, 1953

Fourth Report from the Select Committee on Procedure, H. C. 303, 1964-65

Sixth Report from the Select Committee on Procedure, H. C. 539, 1966-67

INDEX

For Product Safety Concerns and Information please contact our EU
representative GPSR@taylorandfrancis.com
Taylor & Francis Verlag GmbH, Kaufingerstraße 24, 80331 München, Germany